v21618
pc: 184
ISBN's:
   978-1-944607-12-8 (B&W, CB workbook)
   978-1-944607-13-5 (Color Cover, PB workbook)
   978-1-944607-14-2 (eBook)

Articulate Storyline 3 & 360: Beyond the Essentials

"Skills and Drills" Learning

Kevin Siegel & Kal Hadi

iCONLOGiC
"Skills and Drills" Learning

Contents

Notes

iCONLOGiC

"Skills and Drills" Learning

About This Book

This Section Contains Information About:

The Authors

Kevin Siegel is the founder and president of IconLogic, Inc. He has written hundreds of step-by-step computer training books on applications such as *Adobe Captivate, Articulate Storyline, Adobe RoboHelp, Adobe Presenter, Adobe Technical Communication Suite, Adobe Dreamweaver, Adobe InDesign, Microsoft Office, Microsoft PowerPoint, QuarkXPress,* and *TechSmith Camtasia.*

Kevin spent five years in the U.S. Coast Guard as an award-winning photojournalist and has three decades experience as a print publisher, technical writer, instructional designer, and eLearning developer. He is a certified technical trainer, a veteran classroom instructor, and a frequent speaker at trade shows and conventions.

Kevin holds multiple certifications from companies such as Adobe, CompTIA, and the International Council for Certified Online Training Professionals (ICCOTP) as a Certified Online Training Professional (COTP). You can reach Kevin at **ksiegel@iconlogic.com**.

Kal Hadi is a Certified Technical Trainer (CTT) and Certified Online Training Professional (COTP) with more than 20 years of experience in computer graphics, imaging, and electronic publishing. Kal is a graduate of the Rochester Institute of Technology Electronic Publishing graduate program. He is also the author of many books and papers in graphics and web publishing including multiple books on Articulate Storyline.

Book Conventions

People learn by doing. With that simple concept in mind, IconLogic books are created by trainers/authors with years of experience training adult learners. Before IconLogic books, our instructors rarely found a book that was perfect for a classroom setting. If the book was beautiful, odds were that the text was too small to read and hard to follow. If the text in a book was the right size, the quality of exercises left something to be desired.

Finally tiring of using inadequate materials, our instructors started teaching without any books at all. Years ago we had many students ask if the in-class instruction came from a book. If so, they said they'd buy the book. That sparked an idea. We asked students—just like you—what they wanted in a training manual. You responded, and that methodology is used in this book and every IconLogic training manual.

This book has been divided into several modules. Because each module builds on lessons learned in a previous module, we recommend that you complete each module in succession. Each module guides you through lessons step-by-step. Here is the lesson key:

❑ instructions for you to follow will look like this

If you are expected to type anything or if something is important, it is set in bold type like this:

❑ type **9** into the text field

When you are asked to press a key on your keyboard, the instruction looks like this:

❑ press [**shift**]

We hope you enjoy the book. If you have any comments or questions, please see page vi for our contact information.

Confidence Checks

As you move through the lessons in this book, you will come across the little guy at the right. He indicates a Confidence Check. Throughout each module, you will be guided through hands-on, step-by-step exercises. But at some point you'll have to fend for yourself. That is where Confidence Checks come in. Please be sure to complete each of the challenges because some exercises build on completed Confidence Checks.

Book and Storyline System Requirements

This book teaches you how to use either Articulate Storyline 360, which is part of Articulate 360 (a collection of programs available from Articulate via a subscription) or Storyline 3 (which is available for purchase as a standalone product). You can download a free 30-day trial of Storyline or purchase the subscription at **https://articulate.com/360**. You can grab a trial version of the Storyline 3 software from **https://articulate.com/p/storyline-3**.

Once you have installed Articulate 360 you'll have access to Storyline 360. Storyline 3 is a standalone application and you can start it just as you would any program on your computer. According to Articulate, here are the system requirements for using Storyline.

Hardware: CPU, 2.0 GHz processor or higher (32-bit or 64-bit). Memory, 2 GB minimum. Available Disk Space, 1 GB minimum. Display, 1,280 x 800 screen resolution or higher. Multimedia, Sound card, microphone, and webcam to record video and/or narration.

Software: Windows 7 (32-bit or 64-bit), Windows 8 (32-bit or 64-bit), or Windows 10 (32-bit or 64-bit). Mac OS X 10.6.8 or later with Parallels Desktop 7 or later or VMware Fusion 4 or later. .NET 4.5.2 or later (gets installed if not present). Adobe Flash Player 10.3 or later.

Backward Compatibility: Storyline 1 and Storyline 2 projects can be upgraded to Storyline 3 or 360. Storyline 3 and 360 projects cannot be opened or edited with older Storyline versions.

Importing Content: Microsoft PowerPoint 2010 or later (32-bit or 64-bit), Articulate Presenter '09, '13, or 360, Articulate Quizmaker '09, '13, or 360, Articulate Engage '09, '13, or 360.

Publishing to Word: Microsoft Word 2010 or later (32-bit or 64-bit).

Translation: Microsoft Word 2010 or later (32-bit or 64-bit).

Storyline Projects and Assets (Data Files)

You're probably chomping at the bit, ready to dive into Storyline and begin creating eLearning content. As you'll learn as you work through this book, all you need to create eLearning lessons on your own is Articulate Storyline and a little imagination. Wait, you'll also need images... and audio files... the list of supporting assets you'll need could go on and on.

If you have never used Storyline before (and this book assumes you have not), you cannot be expected to learn how to use Storyline on the fly as you create projects. Learning by discovery isn't necessarily a bad thing, but it will take (and possibly waste) a lot of time. We've got a better idea. You provide Storyline (the trial version of the software is fine), and we'll provide all of the project files and supporting assets (such as images and audio files) you need. During the following activity, you will download those assets (data files) from the IconLogic server.

Student Activity: Download Data Files

1. Download the student data files necessary to complete the lessons in this book.

   ❏ start a web browser and visit the following web address:
   http://www.iconlogic.com/pc
   ❏ click the **Articulate Storyline 3 & 360: Beyond the Essentials** link

2. Save the file to your computer. After the file fully downloads, close the web browser.

3. Extract the data files.

   ❏ find the **Storyline3_360BeyondData** file you just downloaded to your computer
   ❏ double-click the file to execute it (even though the file is an EXE file, it's not a program; rather it's an archive containing zipped files)
   ❏ if presented with a Security Warning dialog box, click **Run** or **Yes**

   The WinZip Self Extractor opens.

   ❏ you can **Browse** and **Unzip** the data files anywhere on your computer that you like (**C:** is the default)

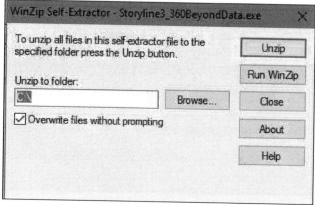

Note: If you changed the **Unzip to Folder** location above, note the location so you can find your files quickly.

☐ click the **Unzip** button

You are notified that several files are unzipped.

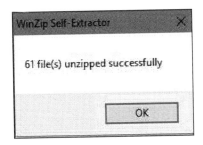

☐ click the **OK** button
☐ click the **Close** button (to close the Extractor)

The data files have been installed on your hard drive (within a folder named **Storyline3_360BeyondData**). As you move through the lessons in this book, you will be working with these files.

How Software Updates Affect This Book

This book was written specifically to teach you how to use Articulate Storyline 3 (perpetual license version) or 360 (subscription version). Because Storyline 360 is part of a subscription to several tools known collectively as Articulate 360, it is expected that Articulate will update the tools frequently.

Some of the updates will likely be minor (bug fixes) and have little or no impact on the lessons in this book. However, Articulate could make significant changes to the Storyline interface, even with seemingly minor updates.

Because it is not feasible for us to modify our books for every Articulate update, some instructions you are asked to follow in this book may not match the updated version of Storyline that you are using. For instance, in the trial version of Storyline, a few items mentioned in this book may require an active subscription and not be available. (We make note of these instances in the book as appropriate.) In addition, the placement of some objects (mainly under the **Insert** and **Format** tabs) may move or the icons could be modified. Nevertheless, you should be able to easily identify the differences between what you see in this book and what you see in the Storyline interface (given that elements remain under the same general categories).

If something on your screen does not match what we show in this book, please visit the Articulate Storyline page on the IconLogic website for possible book updates or errata information (http://www.iconlogic.com/articulate-storyline-360-essentials-workbook.html). Should you get stuck and find no relief on your own (or from our website), feel free to email Kevin or Kal directly for clarification. You can reach Kevin at **ksiegel@iconlogic.com** and Kal at **kal@amananet.com**.

Contacting IconLogic

Web: www.iconlogic.com

Email: info@iconlogic.com

Phone: 410.956.4949

iCONLOGiC

"Skills and Drills" Learning

Rank Your Skills

Before starting this book, complete the skills assessment on the next page.

Skills Assessment

How This Assessment Works

Ten course objectives for *Articulate Storyline 3 & 360: Beyond the Essentials* are listed below. **Before starting the book**, review each objective and rank your skills using the scale next to each objective. A rank of ① means **No Confidence** in the skill. A rank of ⑤ means **Total Confidence**. After you've completed this assessment, work through the entire book. **After finishing the book**, review each objective and rank your skills now that you've completed the book. Most people see dramatic improvements in the second assessment after completing the lessons in this book.

Before-Class Skills Assessment

1. I can create a custom Theme.   ①   ②   ③   ④   ⑤
2. I can create Variables.   ①   ②   ③   ④   ⑤
3. I can create a Motion Path.   ①   ②   ③   ④   ⑤
4. I can add a Trigger to Show a Layer.   ①   ②   ③   ④   ⑤
5. I can add a Cue Point.   ①   ②   ③   ④   ⑤
6. I can change a Character's State based on Time.   ①   ②   ③   ④   ⑤
7. I can create a Randomized Quiz.   ①   ②   ③   ④   ⑤
8. I can execute a Print JavaScript from within Storyline.   ①   ②   ③   ④   ⑤
9. I can set a Tab Order.   ①   ②   ③   ④   ⑤
10. I can add a Keyboard Shortcut to a Button.   ①   ②   ③   ④   ⑤

After-Class Skills Assessment

1. I can create a custom Theme.   ①   ②   ③   ④   ⑤
2. I can create Variables.   ①   ②   ③   ④   ⑤
3. I can create a Motion Path.   ①   ②   ③   ④   ⑤
4. I can add a Trigger to Show a Layer.   ①   ②   ③   ④   ⑤
5. I can add a Cue Point.   ①   ②   ③   ④   ⑤
6. I can change a Character's State based on Time.   ①   ②   ③   ④   ⑤
7. I can create a Randomized Quiz.   ①   ②   ③   ④   ⑤
8. I can execute a Print JavaScript from within Storyline.   ①   ②   ③   ④   ⑤
9. I can set a Tab Order.   ①   ②   ③   ④   ⑤
10. I can add a Keyboard Shortcut to a Button.   ①   ②   ③   ④   ⑤

IconLogic, Inc.
"Skills and Drills" Learning
Web: www.iconlogic.com | Email: info@iconlogic.com

iCONLOGiC
"Skills and Drills" Learning

Module 1: Themes and Templates

In This Module You Will Learn About:

- Themes, page 2
- Templates, page 19

And You Will Learn To:

- Create a Theme, page 2
- Format a Master Slide, page 7
- Create Layouts, page 11
- Save a Theme, page 17
- Load a Theme, page 18
- Add Slide Navigation to the Slide Master, page 19
- Create Variables, page 24
- Add Triggers for a Progress Indicator, page 26
- Create and Use a Template, page 36

Themes

A Theme is a collection of colors, fonts, objects, and master slides. They allow you to maintain a consistent look across slides, scenes, and projects. You can only use a single Theme in a project. However, you can apply custom design properties to master or individual slides throughout a project that supersede default Theme properties.

Student Activity: Create a Theme

1. Create a new project.

   ☐ with Storyline 3 or 360 running, click **New Project** on the Welcome screen

   ☐ at the left of the Storyline **Welcome** screen, click **New Project**

By default, the new project contains a single untitled scene and slide.

2. Observe the appearance of the slide.

   ☐ open the **Untitled Slide** to go to Slide View

Although the slide is blank, it's actually following a default Theme known as "Clean." Observe the bottom of the Storyline window and you'll see the current Theme's name.

This Theme, unless modified, doesn't have anything on the background and uses basic colors and fonts. In the coming steps, you will customize the look of the Theme and save it as a new Theme for future use.

3. Save and customize a Theme.

    ❑ on the **Ribbon**, select the **Design** tab

    ❑ at the right of the **Themes** group, click the **Colors** drop-down menu

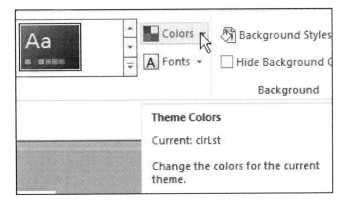

    ❑ from the bottom of the menu, choose **Create New Theme Colors**

    ❑ in the **Name** field, change the name to **Sports**

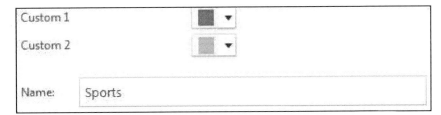

    ❑ spend a few minutes selecting colors from the assorted drop-down menus
    (any colors that you think work well together are fine)

    As you select your colors, you can see how well they work together via the
    Sample at the top right of the dialog box.

    ❑ click the **Save** button

    Note: Choosing colors that work well together isn't as easy as it
    sounds. If colors aren't your thing, no worries. There are websites
    available that will help you select complementary colors. One site that
    we can recommend is **Adobe Colors CC** (https://color.adobe.com/).
    You can change the colors in a Theme at any time by right-clicking the
    Theme name in the Theme Colors drop-down menu and choosing Edit.

4. Test the Theme Colors.

☐ with the slide open, select the **Insert** tab on the **Ribbon**

☐ using the **Shape** tool, draw a shape on the slide

☐ with the shape you just drew selected, click the **Format** tab on the Ribbon

☐ expand the **Shape Styles**

Notice the styles that are available. Each of these colors has come from the Sports Theme you just created. In addition to the Shape Style colors, the colors available for fills and outlines are also based on the Theme colors.

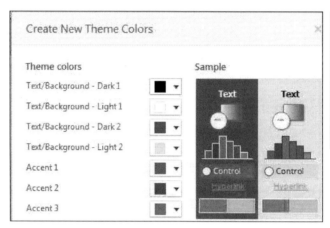
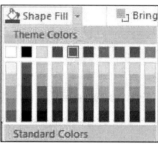

5. Create Theme Fonts.

☐ on the **Ribbon**, select the **Design** tab

☐ to the right of the **Themes** group, click the **Fonts** drop-down menu

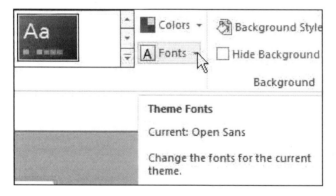

☐ from the bottom of the menu, choose **Create New Theme Fonts**

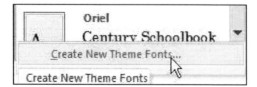

The Create New Themes Fonts dialog box opens.

☐ name the Theme Fonts **Sports**

❏ from the **Heading font** drop-down menu, choose **Arial Black**

❏ from the **Body font** drop-down menu, choose **Arial Rounded MT Bold**

❏ click the **Save** button

Note: Similar to Theme Colors, you can edit the fonts in the Theme Fonts by right-clicking the Theme Fonts name in the Theme Fonts drop-down menu and choosing Edit.

6. Review the Heading and Body font usage on the master slide.

❏ select the **View** tab on the **Ribbon**

❏ from the **Views** group, click **Slide Master**

❏ click the **Master Slide** (the first slide)

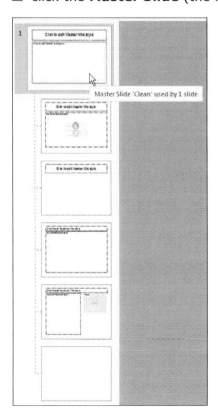

Notice that the Master Slide is using the two fonts you specified for the Heading and the Body.

Click to edit Master title style

Click to edit Master text styles

Student Activity: Format a Master Slide

1. Add a background image to the slide master.

   ❒ still working on the **Slide Master** (the top slide, which is known as the **parent**), click **Format Background**

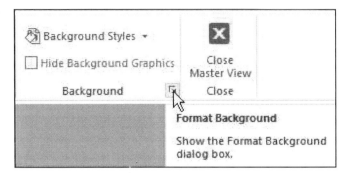

   The Format Background dialog box opens.

   ❒ from the **Fill** area, select **Picture or texture fill**

   ❒ from the **Insert from** area, click the **File** button

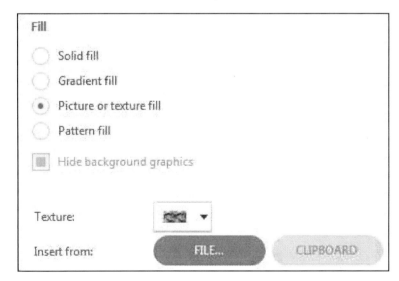

   Note: If you have not yet downloaded and installed the **Storyline3_360BeyondData** files that support the lessons in this book, turn to the **About This Book Section** and complete the "Download Data Files" activity that begins on page iv before moving forward.

   ❒ from the **Storyline3_360BeyondData**, open the **assets** folder

   ❒ open **sports-field-bg**

   ❒ click the **Close** button

   The image is instantly added to all of the slides. The image is a bit too dark, so you'll change its transparency next.

2. Increase the transparency of a background image.

   ❏ at the left of the Storyline window, right-click the parent slide and choose **Format Background**

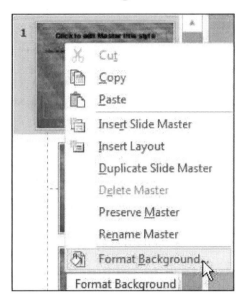

The Format Background dialog box reopens.

   ❏ from the bottom of the dialog box, drag the **Transparency** slider **right** to **25%**

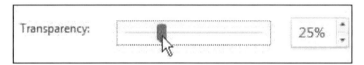

Note: The higher the transparency, the less of the background image you will see on the slide. If you had made the transparency 100%, the image would have disappeared from the slide completely.

   ❏ click the **Close** button

3. Use a keyboard shortcut to add a logo to the slide master.

   ❏ press [**ctrl**] [**j**] on your keyboard

The **Insert Picture** dialog box opens. (If keyboard shortcuts aren't you're thing, you could insert an image via the **Insert** tab on the **Ribbon**.)

   ❏ from the **Storyline3_360BeyondData**, **assets** folder, open **sports-logo**

Master Slide Confidence Check

1. Still working on the parent slide master, resize and reposition the logo you just imported until your slide looks similar to the image below.

2. Increase the transparency of the image by **50%**.

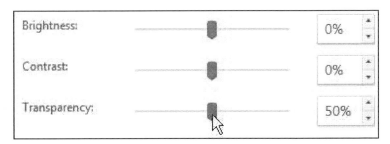

3. Delete both of the text placeholders from the parent slide master.

4. Insert a Text Box on the parent slide master.

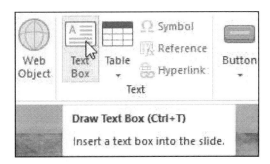

5. With the Text Box selected, click the **Insert** tab on the Ribbon.

6. From the **Text** group, click **Symbol**.

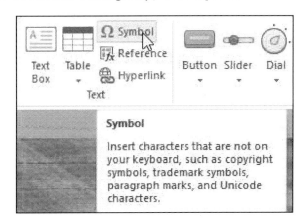

7. Select **Arial Rounded MT Bold** as the Font.

8. Select the **Copyright symbol** and then click **Insert**.

9. Add the following text after the Copyright symbol: **Rules of the Game**.

10. Change the font size used in the Text Box to **10**.

11. Change the font color to **white**.

12. Change the paragraph alignment to **Right**.

13. Drag the text box to the lower right of the slide.

14. Close the Master View.

15. If there are any previously drawn shapes on slide one, delete them.

16. Save the project as **MyDesign** and then close it.

Student Activity: Create Layouts

1. Open the **ThemeMe** project from the **Storyline3_360BeyondData** folder.

   This project looks exactly like the project you just closed.

2. Delete the existing Layout Master Slides.

   ❏ select the **View** tab on the Ribbon

   ❏ from the **Views** group, click **Slide Master**

   ❏ press the [**ctrl**] key on your keyboard and select slides **2**, **3**, **4**, and **5** (only the parent master and blank slide master should be deselected)

   ❏ release the [**ctrl**] key

   ❏ select the **Slide Master** tab on the Ribbon

   ❏ from the **Edit Master** group, click **Delete**

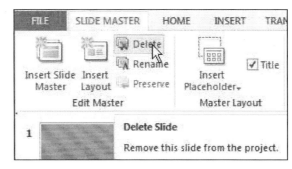

3. Duplicate a layout master slide.

❏ right-click the second slide and choose **Duplicate Layout**

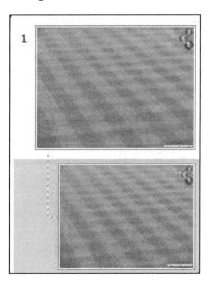

4. Rename the duplicate layout master slide.

❏ right-click the third slide and choose **Rename Layout**

The Rename dialog box opens.

❏ change the name of the layout to **Lesson Introduction**

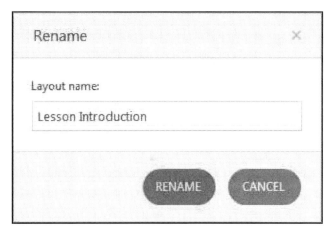

❏ click the **Rename** button

The new name does not appear on the layout. However, if you hover above the layout, you'll see its name. The name will prove valuable later when you apply a layout to a slide.

5. Enable the guides.

   ❑ select the **View** tab on the **Ribbon**

   ❑ from the **Grid and Guides** group, click **Guides**

   Two guides appear on the layout. You will be able to use these next when inserting a placeholder.

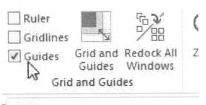

6. Insert a placeholder.

   ❑ select the **Slide Master** tab on the **Ribbon**

   ❑ from the **Master Layout** group, click the **Insert Placeholder** drop-down menu

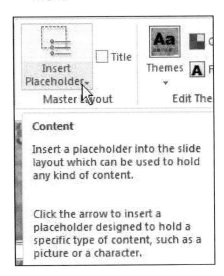

   ❑ choose **Picture**

   ❑ drag a large vertical placeholder beginning in the top left corner of the **Lesson Introduction** layout that takes up half of the slide

   A placeholder is a unique kind of object that can be added only to a master slide layout. When you apply a master slide layout that contains a placeholder object to a project slide, the placeholder can easily be replaced with appropriate content. When you add a standard object (such as a logo) to a master slide layout, the object appears but is not editable.

   Note: Placeholders cannot be added to the Parent master slide.

7. Format the placeholder.

☐ right-click the placeholder and choose **Format Shape**

☐ select the **Line Color** category

☐ from the **Line Color** area, select **Solid line**

☐ from the **Color** area, choose **White**

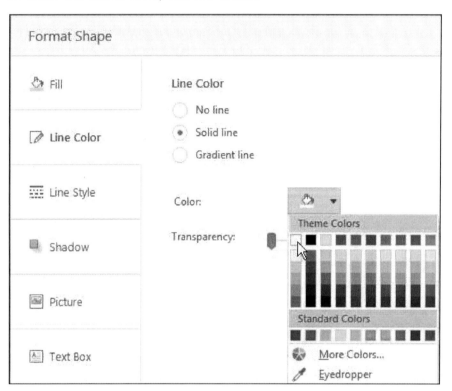

☐ select the **Line Style** category

☐ from the **Width** drop-down menu, choose **10px**

☐ click the **Close** button

Custom Layouts Confidence Check

1. Still working on the **ThemeMe** project, the **Lesson Introduction** layout, right-click the picture placeholder and choose **Size and Position**.

2. With the **Position** category selected, change the **Horizontal** to **5** and then change the **Vertical** to **5**.

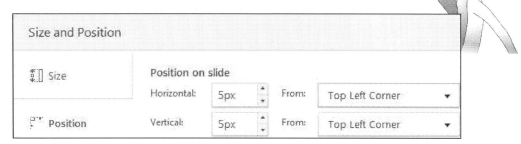

3. Select the **Size** category and change the Height to **530**; the **Width** to **350**. (Click the **Close** button when finished.)

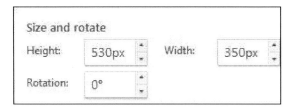

4. Insert a **Text Placeholder** onto the Lesson Introduction layout.

5. With the Text Placeholder selected, replace the existing text with **Click to enter RULE title**.

6. Change the text and object attributes as you see fit; move and resize the placeholders until your layout looks similar to the image below.

7. Duplicate the **Lesson Introduction** layout and name it **Rule**.

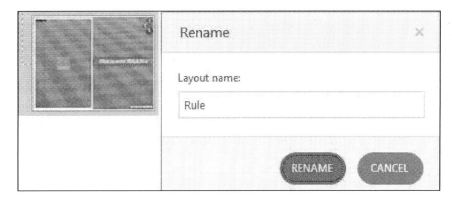

8. Edit the Rule layout so that it is similar to the image below.

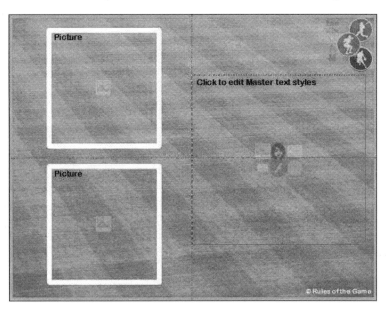

9. Close the Master View.

Student Activity: Save a Theme

1. Ensure that the **ThemeMe** project is still open.

2. Save a Theme.

   ☐ select the **Design** tab on the **Ribbon**

   ☐ from the right side of the **Themes** group, click to **Expand** the project Themes

   ☐ from the bottom of the Themes list, click **Save Current Theme**

   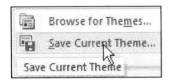

   ☐ name the Theme **sports**

   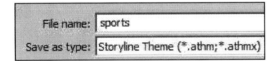

   Note: The file is automatically given an **athmx** extension for use with Storyline projects.

   ☐ browse to the **Storyline3_360BeyondData** folder

   ☐ click the **Save** button

3. Save and close the ThemeMe project.

Student Activity: Load a Theme

1. Create a New project.

2. Load a Theme.

   ❐ select the **Design** tab on the **Ribbon**

   ❐ from the right side of the **Themes** group, click to **Expand** the project Themes

   Notice that the sports theme you saved a moment ago isn't listed among your Themes.

   ❐ from the bottom of the Themes list, click **Browse for Themes**

   ![Browse for Themes menu]
   Browse for Themes...
   Browse for Themes Theme...

   ❐ browse to the **Storyline3_360BeyondData** folder

   ❐ open the **sports** Theme

   Two things happen within your project. First, the lone slide in your project takes on the look of the Theme. Second, the **sports** Theme and its layouts are now a part of the new project.

3. Apply Theme layouts to slides.

   ❐ open slide **1.1**

   ❐ right-click the slide and choose **Apply Layout > Lesson Introduction**

   The slide immediately takes on the look of the Lesson Introduction layout.

4. Close the project without saving.

Templates

A Storyline template is a master file that allows you to create lessons that are consistent from project to project. Typical templates include such things as layouts, content areas, variables, animations, navigation, and more.

Student Activity: Add Slide Navigation to the Slide Master

1. Open the **TemplateMe1** project from the **Storyline3_360BeyondData** folder.

2. Go to Slide Master View.

3. Select the **Lesson Introduction** Layout. (The third slide.)

4. Use a keyboard shortcut to insert an image.

   ❏ press [**ctrl**] [**j**] on your keyboard

   The Insert Picture dialog box opens.

   ❏ from the **Storyline3_360BeyondData**, open the **assets** folder
   ❏ open **continue-arrow**

5. Position the continue-arrow image similar to the picture below.

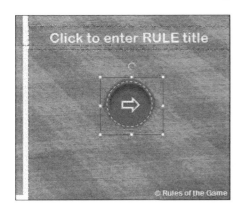

6. Give the image a name.

   ❏ with the continue-arrow image selected, go to the **Timeline** and change the name of the image to **Continue Button**

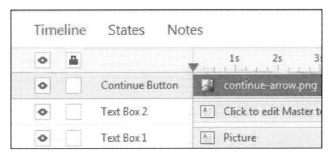

7. Add a Trigger that takes learners to the next slide when they click the **Continue** button.

   ☐ with the **Continue Button** selected, go to the **Triggers** panel and click **Create a new trigger**

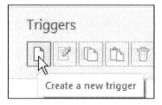

The Trigger Wizard opens.

   ☐ ensure that the **Action** is set to **Jump to slide**

   ☐ click the **OK** button

The new Trigger appears on the Triggers panel.

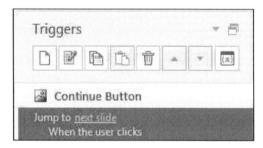

8. Add a Trigger that plays a sound when learners hover above the **Continue Button**.

   ☐ with the **Continue Button** selected, go to the **Triggers** panel and click **Create a new trigger**

   ☐ change the **Action** to **Play Media**

   ☐ from the **Media** drop-down menu, choose **Audio from File**

❑ from the **assets** folder, open the **audio** folder

❑ open **hover-sound**

You should be back in the Trigger Wizard.

❑ from the **When** drop-down menu, choose **Mouse hovers over**

❑ from the **Object** drop-down menu, ensure **Continue Button** is selected

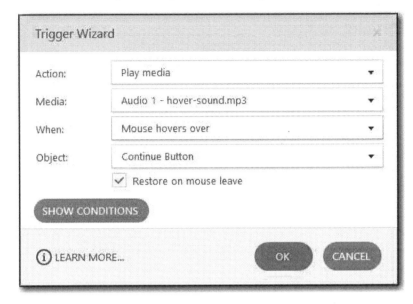

❑ click the **OK** button

9. Save your work.

Navigation Confidence Check

1. Still working in the **TemplateMe1** project, and in the **Slide Master** View, select the **Rule** layout.

2. Add the following images (from the assets folder) to the layout:

   next-arrow

   previous-arrow

3. Position the images so that your Rule layout looks similar to this:

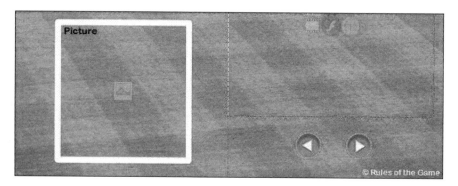

4. Name the two images as follows:

   Next Button

   Previous Button

5. Create a new Trigger for each button. The Next button should **Jump** the learner to the **next** slide; the Previous Button should **Jump** the learner to the **previous** slide.

6. Add a Trigger to each button that plays the **click-sound** audio file (located in the assets folder) when the learner clicks either button.

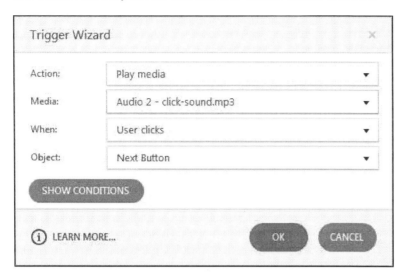

7. Close the Slide Master View.

   Notice that the first slide in the Scene is already using the Lesson Introduction Layout. As such, the slide already has the **Continue Button**.

8. Insert **four** more slides to the Scene that use the **Rule** layout.

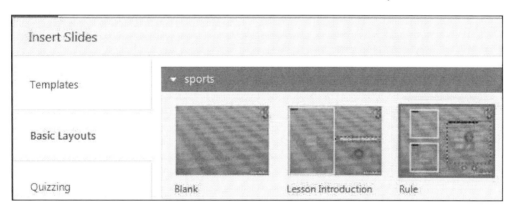

9. Insert **one** more slide to the Scene that uses the **Blank** layout.

10. Close any open slides.

11. Save and close the project.

Student Activity: Create Variables

1. Open the **TemplateMe2** project from the **Storyline3_360BeyondData** folder.

2. Create a Variable.

   ☐ on the **Triggers** panel, click **Manage project variables**

   The **Variables** dialog box opens. If you worked through the first book in this series ("*Articulate Storyline 3 & 360: The Essentials*"), you learned that Variables serve as buckets for data. The data can be used to provide feedback to the learner and/or allow you as the developer to create conditional scenarios. For instance, you could use a variable to capture a learners name. Once the name has been "stored" by the variable, the name can be displayed over and over again throughout the lesson. In a gaming scenario, variables allow you to calculate the score for each player. They also allow you to display content based on a certain set of conditions. When those conditions are met, an image appears or a video plays. You are going to use Variables in your Template project that will control a Progress indicator you are adding.

   ☐ from the lower left of the Variables dialog box, click **Create a new variable**

   ☐ name the new Variable **rule1** and then, from the **Type** drop-down menu, choose **True/False**

   ☐ from the **Value** drop-down menu, choose **False**

   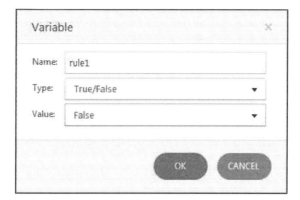

   ☐ click the **OK** button

Navigation Confidence Check

1. Still working in the **TemplateMe2** project and in the **Variables** dialog box, create **three** more Variables called **rule2**, **rule3**, and **rule4**.

2. For each new **Variable**, the Type should be **True/False** and the Value should be **False**.

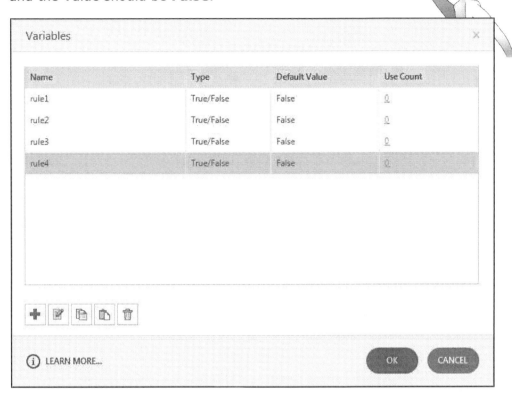

3. Create another new Variable named **progress**.

4. Change the Type to **Number** and ensure that the Value is **0**. (Click the OK button when finished.)

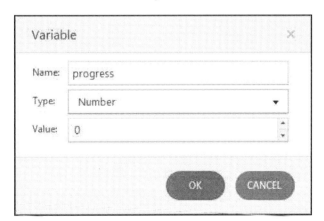

Student Activity: Add Triggers for a Progress Indicator

1. Ensure that the **TemplateMe2** project is still open.

2. Explore the states that have been added to an object.

   ☐ open slide **1.2**

   On the Pasteboard to the left of the slide, notice that there is an object that we've created for you (named **progress**).

   ☐ select the **progress** object and, from the bottom of the **Storyline** window, click **States** (located to the right of **Timeline**)

   Notice that the object has five States: Normal, 25%, 50%, 75%, and 100%. During the steps that follow, you will move the object to the slide, and then you will program the object using Triggers and the Variables you created earlier so that the states automatically change based on how the learner navigates through the lesson.

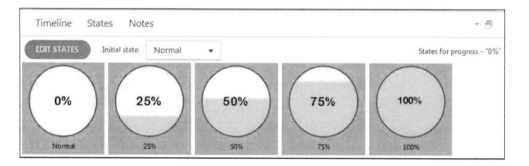

3. Drag the **progress** object onto the slide similar to the image below.

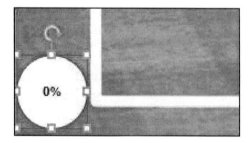

4. Add a Trigger to slide **1.2** that will change the **rule1** Variable from **False** to **True**.

□ ensure that nothing on slide 1.2 is selected

□ on the **Triggers** panel, click **Create a new trigger**

□ from the **Action** drop-down menu, choose **Adjust variable**

□ from the **Variable** drop-down menu, choose **rule1**

□ from the **Operator** drop-down menu, choose **= Assignment**

□ change the **Value** to **Value**

□ from the next drop-down menu to the right, change the value to **True**

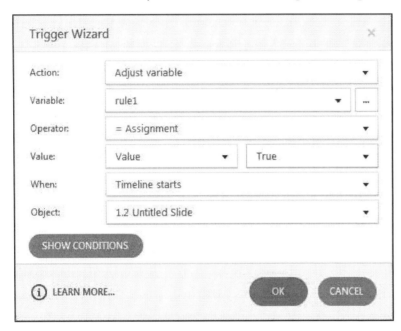

□ click the **OK** button

Next you will add another Trigger that will increment the **progress** variable you created earlier. This Trigger is necessary to ensure that each slide counts only once toward the learner's overall progress.

5. Add a Trigger to increment the progress number variable.

    ❏ ensure that nothing on slide **1.2** is selected

    ❏ on the **Triggers** panel, click **Create a new trigger**

    ❏ from the **Action** drop-down menu, choose **Adjust variable**

    ❏ from the **Variable** drop-down menu, choose **progress**

    ❏ from the **Operator** drop-down menu, choose **+ Add**

    ❏ change the **Value** to **Value**

    ❏ from the next drop-down menu to the right, change the value to **1**

Trigger Wizard		×
Action:	Adjust variable	▼
Variable:	progress	▼ ⋯
Operator:	+ Add	▼
Value:	Value ▼	1 ▲▼
When:	Timeline starts	▼
Object:	1.2 Untitled Slide	▼
SHOW CONDITIONS		
ⓘ LEARN MORE...	OK	CANCEL

❏ from the bottom of the Trigger Wizard, click **Show Conditions**

❏ from the lower right of the dialog box, click **Add a new "AND" or "OR" condition**

The On Condition dialog box opens.

❏ from the **If** drop-down menu, choose **rule1**

❏ from the **Operator** drop-down menu, choose **==Equal to**

❏ from the **Type** drop-down menu, choose **Value**

❏ leave the **Value** set to **False**

❏ click the **OK** button

On Condition:
rule1 == Equal to False

❏ click the **OK** button

Next you will add a Trigger that will change the state of the progress object from 0% to 25% *if* the learner visits the slide.

6. Add a Trigger that changes the State of the progress object.

   ❏ ensure that nothing on slide **1.2** is selected

   ❏ on the **Triggers** panel, click **Create a new trigger**

   ❏ from the **Action** drop-down menu, choose **Change state of**

   ❏ from the **On Object** drop-down menu, choose **progress**

   ❏ from the **To State** drop-down menu, choose **25%**

7. Make the Trigger Conditional.

   ❏ from the bottom of the Trigger Wizard, click **Show Conditions**

   ❏ from the lower right of the dialog box, click **Add a new "AND" or "OR" condition**

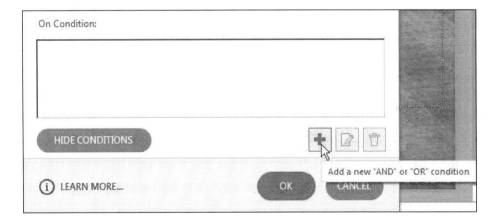

   ❏ from the **If** drop-down menu, choose **progress**

   ❏ from the **Operator** drop-down menu, choose **== Equal to**

   ❏ from the **Type** drop-down menu, choose **Value**

❏ ensure that the **Value** set to **1**

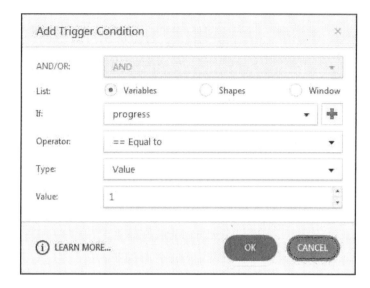

❏ click the **OK** button twice to close both dialog boxes

8. Reorder the Triggers.

❏ select the **Add 1.00 to progress When the timeline starts...**Trigger and click the **Move the selected trigger** tool to move the Trigger into **first** position

❏ select the **Set rule1 equal to True...** Trigger and click the **Move the selected trigger** tool to move the Trigger into **second** position

❏ select the **Change state of progress - "0%" to 25%...** Trigger and click the **Move the selected trigger** tool to move the Trigger into **third** position

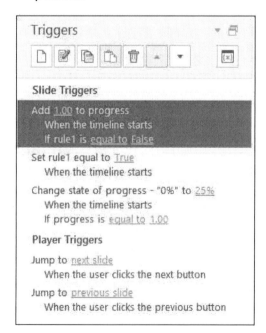

9. Preview the project.

10. Click the **Continue** button on the first slide.

   Once you are on the second slide, the **progress** object should show 25% because you have viewed one of the four remaining slides (the introduction slide was intentionally left out of the progress).

11. Close the preview.

12. Add more Triggers.

   ☐ go to slide **1.3** and ensure that nothing on the slide is selected

   ☐ on the **Triggers** panel, click **Create a new trigger**

   ☐ from the **Action** drop-down menu, choose **Adjust variable**

   ☐ from the **Variable** drop-down menu, choose **progress**

   ☐ from the **Operator** drop-down menu, choose **+ Add**

   ☐ change the **Value** to **Value**

   ☐ from the next drop-down menu to the right, change the value to **1**

   ☐ from the **When** drop-down menu, choose **Timeline starts**

   ☐ from the bottom of the Trigger Wizard, click **Show Conditions**

   ☐ from the lower right of the dialog box, click **Add a new "AND" or "OR" condition**

   The Add Trigger Condition dialog box opens.

   ☐ from the **If** drop-down menu, choose **rule2**

   ☐ from the **Operator** drop-down menu, choose **==Equal to**

   ☐ from the **Type** drop-down menu, choose **Value**

   ☐ leave the Value set to **False**

❏ click the **OK** button

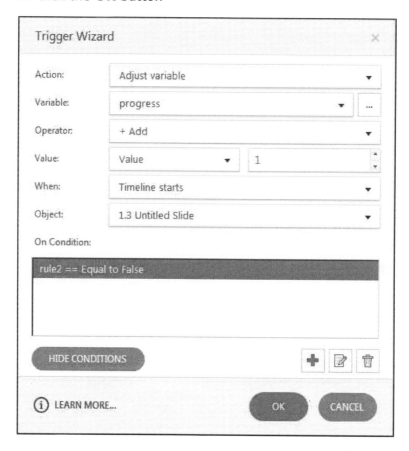

❏ click the **OK** button

❏ still working on slide **1.3,** ensure that nothing is selected and, on the **Triggers** panel, click **Create a new trigger**

❏ from the **Action** drop-down menu, choose **Adjust variable**

❏ from the **Variable** drop-down menu, choose **rule2**

❏ from the **Operator** drop-down menu, choose **= Assignment**

The **rule2** Variable has a default value of false. The Trigger changes its value to True.

❏ change the **Value** to **Value**

❒ from the next drop-down menu to the right, choose **True**

❒ click the **OK** button

❒ go back to slide **1.2**

❒ on the **Triggers** panel, click **Create a new trigger**

❒ from the **Action** drop-down menu, choose **Change state of**

❒ from the **On Object** drop-down menu, choose **progress**

❒ from the **To State** drop-down menu, choose **50%**

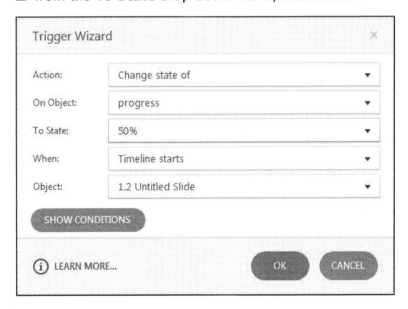

❒ from the bottom of the Trigger Wizard, click **Show Conditions**

❒ from the lower right of the dialog box, click **Add a new "AND" or "OR" condition**

❒ from the **If** drop-down menu, choose **progress**

❏ from the **Operator** drop-down menu, choose **==Equal to**

❏ from the **Type** drop-down menu, choose **Value**

❏ change the **Value** to **2**

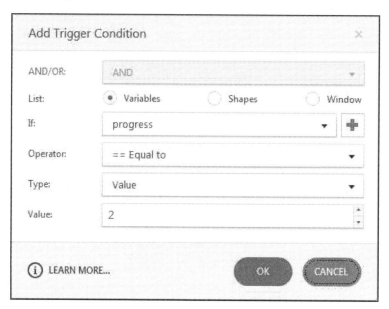

❏ click the **OK** button

❏ click the **OK** button

13. Preview the entire project.

14. Click the **Continue** button on the first slide.

    Once you are on the second slide, the **progress** object should again show 25%.

15. Click the Next button to go to the next slide.

16. Click the Previous button to return to slide 1.2.

    Because you have visited slides 1.2 and 1.3 (50% of the required slides), the Progress indicator displays 50%.

17. Save and close the project.

Student Activity: Create and Use a Template

1. Open the **TemplateMe3** project from the **Storyline3_360BeyondData** folder.

2. Preview the project.

   As you go from slide to slide, notice that this project is similar to the project you just closed. The Progress indicator States and Triggers have been added to slides 1.3, 1.4, and 1.5. The Progress indicator works even when you jump around the lesson.

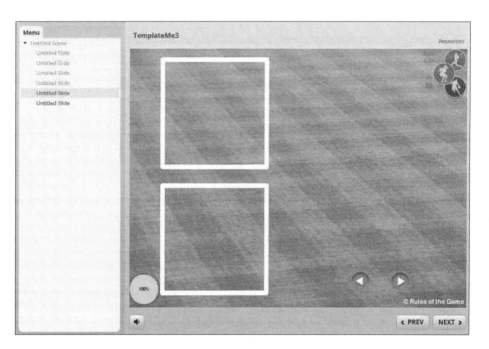

3. Save a project as a Template.

   ❏ choose **File > Save As**

   ❏ change the name to **SportRulesTemplate**

   ❏ from the **Save as type** drop-down menu, choose **Storyline Template**

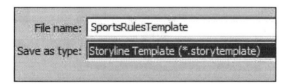

   ❏ ensure that you are saving to the **Storyline3_360BeyondData** folder

   ❏ click the **Save** button

   Notice that the project gets a **.storylinetemplate** extension (as opposed to a .story extension found on standard Storyline projects).

4. Close the template.

---

5. Create a new project based on a template.

    ❑ from the Storyline Welcome screen, click **Import**

    ❑ choose **Import from story template**

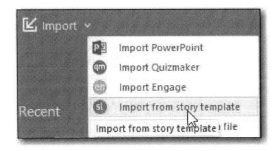

    ❑ from the **Storyline3_360BeyondData** folder, open
      SportRulesTemplate

    The Insert Slides dialog box opens.

    ❑ select all of the slides (you can select multiple slides pressing [**shift**] on
      your keyboard and clicking the slides)

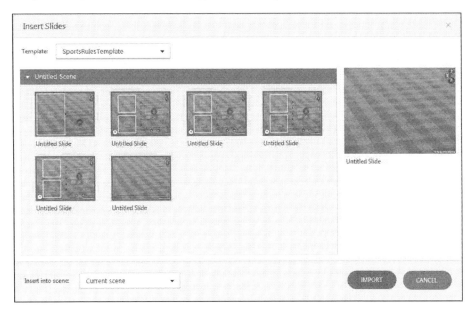

    ❑ click the **Import** button

    The new project has all of the slides, Triggers, Layers, Variables, placeholders,
    slide masters, and layouts in the template. And just like that, you are ready to
    work on the lesson's content. If you use the template, any projects you create
    from this point forward will have a consistent look and feel.

6. Close the project without saving.

7. Review a project created with the Template.

❑ from the **Storyline3_360BeyondData** folder, open **golf-rules**

❑ preview the project

This project was built using the same **SportRulesTemplate** you learned to create during this module. After basing the project on the template, we went through and added the images, animation, and text. Because we already had the template, building the final project took approximately 30 minutes.

8. Close the Preview.

9. Close the project.

iCONLOGiC

"Skills and Drills" Learning

Module 2: Custom Navigation

In This Module You Will Learn About:

And You Will Learn To:

Motion Paths

Although it's easy to add animations to an object that allow for simple movement, Motion Paths allow you to move slide objects from one location to another along complex paths. Unlike simple animations, you can apply multiple Motion Paths to an object. In addition, Motion Paths can be associated with Triggers to initiate an object's motion along a path.

Student Activity: Preview a Completed Custom Menu

1. Open **FinishedCustomMenu** from the **Storyline3_360BeyondData** folder.

2. Open slide **1.6**.

3. Preview the Slide.

4. Click each of the golf balls at the bottom of the screen.

5. Notice that as you click, the images go up or down along a Motion Path. In addition, each image is associated with a layer containing specific text.

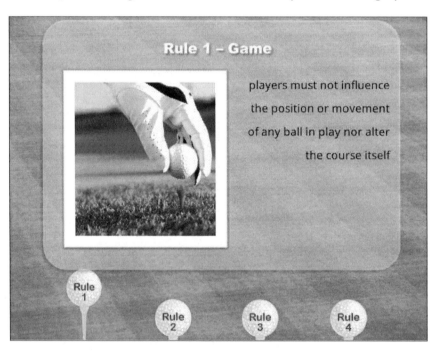

During the lessons that follow, you will learn how to add the Motion Paths and Triggers required to make the slide interaction work.

6. Close the Preview.

7. Close the project.

Student Activity: Create a Motion Path

1. Open **CustomMenuMe** from the **Storyline3_360BeyondData** folder.

2. Open slide **1.6**.

3. Add a Motion Path to an image.

   ❏ on the slide, select the **Rule 1** ball image

   ❏ on the **Ribbon**, select the **Animations** tab

   ❏ from the **Motion Paths** group, click **Add Motion Path**

   ❏ from the **Basic** section, click **Lines**

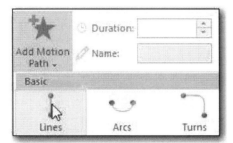

On the slide, notice that a few things have changed about the ball image. First, there's a star in the upper left of the image indicating that an animation is associated with the image. Second, there is a line in the middle of the image—this is the Motion Path. Third, the Motion Path has a green circle indicating the default origin of the Motion Path. Fourth, the red circle at the bottom of the Motion Path indicates the end point of the path.

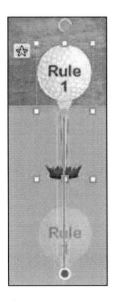

4. Deselect the Rule 1 image.

   With the image deselected, notice that you can still see the Motion Path. However, the beginning and ending points are not as prominent.

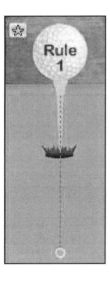

5. Preview the Slide.

   By default, a Trigger has been associated with the Motion Path. The Trigger is making the Rule 1 image move downward off the slide.

6. Close the Preview.

Student Activity: Change Motion Path Options

1. Ensure that the **CustomMenuMe** project is still open and that you're working on slide **1.6**.

2. Change the options for the Motion Path.

   ☐ on the **Rule 1** image, click the dotted line of the **Motion Path** to select it

   A selected Motion Path has the green and red circle as opposed to the triangles.

   ☐ from the **Motion Paths** group on the **Animations** tab, click **Path Options**

   ☐ change the direction to **Up**

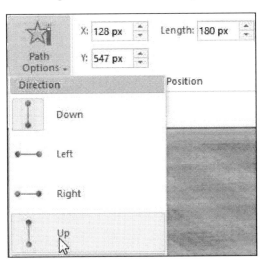

3. Preview the Slide.

   The Rule 1 image now moves upward. It's way too high, in fact; something you'll fix next.

4. Close the Preview.

5. Adjust the ending point of a Motion Path.

   ☐ on the **Motion Path**, position your mouse over the red ending point

   ☐ press [**shift**] on your keyboard

   ☐ with [**shift**] pressed, **drag** the red ending point down until the top of the golf ball lines up with the horizontal guide

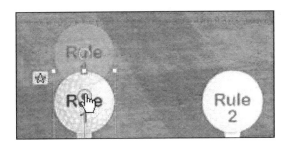

❒ release the mouse and then the [**shift**] key

6. Preview the Slide.

The Rule 1 image still moves upward. But this time, the animation ends much lower on the slide. The problem now is that the speed of the animation is a little slow. You'll speed things up a bit next.

7. Close the Preview.

Student Activity: Change the Duration of a Motion Path

1. Ensure that the **CustomMenuMe** project is still open and that you're working on slide **1.6**.

2. Speed up the Duration of a Motion Path.

   ☐ on the **Rule 1** image, select the **Motion Path**

   ☐ from the **Motion Paths** group on the **Animations** tab, **Motion Paths** group, change the **Duration** to **1.00** (1 second)

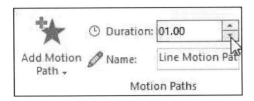

3. Preview the Slide.

   As the animation occurs, notice this time that the speed is a bit slower than before.

4. Close the Preview.

Student Activity: Add a Second Motion Path to an Object

1. Ensure that the **CustomMenuMe** project is still open and that you're working on slide **1.6**.

2. Select the **Rule 1** image (**not the Motion Path**).

   If you're not sure if you've selected the image or the Motion Path, it's often easier to select an object using the Timeline. The image you need to select is called **rule1-golf-png**.

3. Add a second Motion Path.

   ☐ on the **Ribbon**, **Animations** tab, click **Add Motion Path**

   ☐ from the **Basic** group, click **Lines**

   It's not easy to tell, but the image now has two Motion Paths. The first Motion Path is short. The new Motion Path is longer with an end point well below the slide.

4. Preview the Slide.

   The newest Motion Path takes precedence—the image goes down and off the slide. Notice that the first Motion Path doesn't come into play.

5. Close the Preview.

6. Observe the Triggers panel.

On the Triggers panel, notice that Triggers have been added that move the object along each path when the Timeline starts. The Triggers are automatically named sequentially: Line Motion Path 1 and Line Motion Path 2. The reason the second Motion Path is usurping the first one is that it's newer.

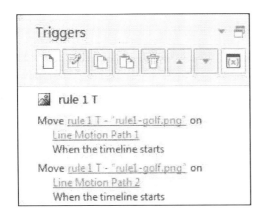

This slide is going to contain several Motion Paths (two for each ball image). As each ball is clicked by the learner, the other balls need to return to their original positions. Next you will edit the ending point for the second Motion Path that will ensure the ball returns to its original position.

7. Edit the new Motion Path.

❏ on the newer Motion Path, position your mouse over the red ending point

❏ press [**shift**] on your keyboard

❏ with [**shift**] pressed, **drag** the red ending point **up** until the shaded golf ball is as lined up with the original golf ball as you can get it

❏ release the mouse and then the [**shift**] key

Note: You can use your keyboard to nudge an object a few pixels at a time. When you press the arrow keys on your keyboard, the selected object (or Motion Path) moves 10 pixels. When you press [**ctrl**] on your keyboard and then the arrow keys, the selected object moves 1 pixel. You may find this particularly useful when trying to align the two Motion Paths.

Motion Path Confidence Check

1. Still working on slide **1.6** of the **CustomMenuMe** project, add two new Motion Paths to the **Rule 2** image.

2. The Duration for each Motion Path should be **1** second.

3. The first Motion should make the ball go up; the second Motion Path should be shortened so that it returns the second ball to its original position... just like the first ball image.

4. Add two new Motion Paths to the **Rule 3** image.

5. The first Motion should make the ball go up; the second Motion Path should be shortened so that it returns the second ball to its original position... just like the first ball image.

6. Add two new Motion Paths to the **Rule 4** image.

7. The first Motion should make the ball go up; the second Motion Path should be shortened so that it returns the second ball to its original position... just like the first ball image.

8. Save and close the project.

Triggers and Motion Paths

During the last several activities, you added eight Motion Paths to a project. As you added each Motion Path, a Trigger was also added to the Triggers panel that instructed the Motion Path to activate when the slide's Timeline starts. In the activities that follow, you'll remove the original Triggers and add your own that will activate the Motion Paths when each ball is clicked by the learner.

Student Activity: Delete Specific Triggers

1. Open **CustomMenuMe2** from the **Storyline3_360BeyondData** folder.

2. Open slide **1.6**.

3. Delete the second Motion Path Trigger for each image.

   ❏ on the **Triggers** panel, select the Trigger that ends with **Motion Path 2**

   ❏ at the top of the Triggers panel, click **Delete**

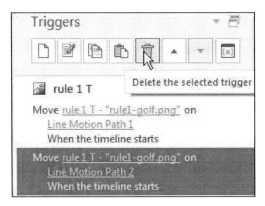

   ❏ click the **Yes** button

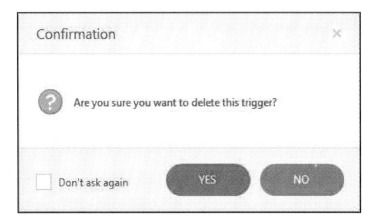

You've deleted the Trigger (the thing that makes the Motion Path activate), but not the Motion Path itself.

   ❏ on the **Triggers** panel, select the Trigger that ends with **Motion Path 4**

   ❏ at the top of the Triggers panel, click **Delete**

Again, you've deleted the Trigger, but not the Motion Path.

❏ click the **Yes** button

❏ on the **Triggers** panel, select the Trigger that ends with **Motion Path 6**

❏ at the top of the Triggers panel, click **Delete**

❏ click the **Yes** button

❏ on the **Triggers** panel, select the Trigger that ends with **Motion Path 8**

❏ at the top of the Triggers panel, click **Delete**

❏ click the **Yes** button

4. Preview the Slide.

All of the images rise up on the slide. Next, you'll edit the Triggers so the images don't rise automatically... but only when clicked by the learner.

5. Close the Preview.

Student Activity: Edit "When" a Trigger Occurs

1. Ensure that the **CustomMenuMe2** project is still open and that you're working on slide **1.6**.

2. Edit a Trigger so that the Rule 1 image does not go up until clicked by the leaner.

   ❑ on the **Triggers** panel, select the Trigger ending with the words **Motion Path 1**

   ❑ at the top of the **Triggers** panel, click **Edit the selected trigger**

   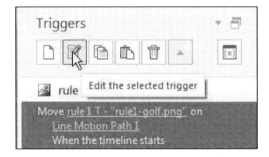

   The Trigger Wizard opens.

   ❑ from the **When** drop-down menu, choose **User clicks**

   ❑ from the **Object** drop-down menu, ensure **rule 1 T** is selected

   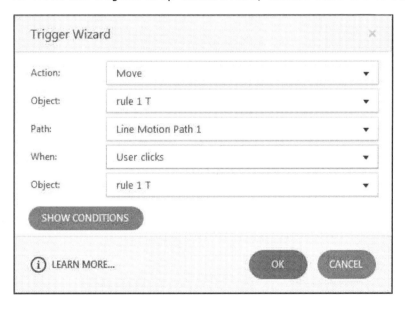

   ❑ click the **OK** button

3. Preview the Slide.

   All of the images except the first one automatically rise up on the slide. The first image rises only when clicked.

4. Close the Preview.

Editing Triggers Confidence Check

1. Still working in the CustomMenuMe2 project, edit the remaining three Triggers so that the remaining images rise only when clicked.

2. Preview the slide.

   Each image should rise only when clicked.

3. Close the preview.

4. Save and close the project.

Triggers and States

During the last Confidence Check, you created Triggers that allowed the golf ball images to rise only when the learner clicks on them. However, as the learner moves from one ball to the next, the previous balls clicked remain up. Because each ball shows a unique layer containing text, you need the previously clicked balls to be reset.

Student Activity: Add Triggers that Reset Motion Paths

1. Open **CustomMenuMe3** from the **Storyline3_360BeyondData** folder.

2. Open slide **1.6**.

   Each of the ball images on the slide are associated with Motion Paths. You added the Motion Paths during previous activities in this module. Their job is to reset the position of the balls to their original position.

3. Add a Trigger that resets a Motion Path.

   ❑ select the **Rule 1** image

   ❑ on the Triggers panel, click **Create a new trigger**

   The Trigger Wizard dialog box opens.

   ❑ from the **Actions** drop-down menu, choose **Move**

   ❑ from the **Object** drop-down menu, choose **rule 2 T** (this is the image of the ball and tee immediately to the right of the image you selected)

   ❑ from the **Path** drop-down menu, choose **Line Motion Path 4**

   ❑ from the **When** drop-down menu, ensure **User clicks** is selected

   ❑ from the **Object** drop-down menu, ensure **rule 1 T** is selected

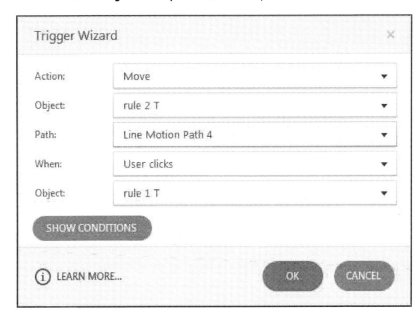

   ❑ click the **OK** button

4. Preview the slide.

5. Click the **Rule 2** image.

   The image rises as expected.

6. Click the **Rule 1** image.

   Thanks to the Trigger you just added, the Rule 2 image goes back to its original position.

7. Close the Preview and then save your work.

8. Ensure that you're still working on slide 1.6 of the **CustomMenuMe3** project.

9. Add another Trigger that resets a Motion Path.

   ❑ select the **Rule 1** image

   ❑ on the Triggers panel, click **Create a new trigger**

   The Trigger Wizard dialog box reopens.

   ❑ from the **Actions** drop-down menu, choose **Move**

   ❑ from the **Object** drop-down menu, choose **rule 3 T**

   ❑ from the **Path** drop-down menu, choose **Line Motion Path 6**

   ❑ from the **When** drop-down menu, ensure **User clicks** is selected

   ❑ from the **Object** drop-down menu, ensure **rule 1 T** is selected

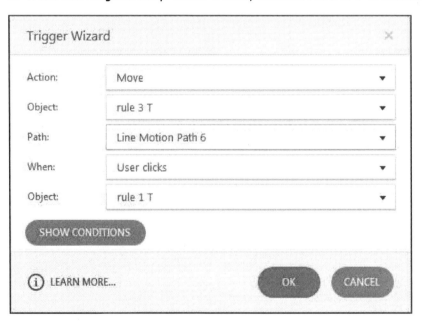

   ❑ click the **OK** button

10. Preview the slide.

11. Click the Rule 2 and Rule 3 images.

    Both images rise as expected.

12. Click the Rule 1 image to reset the motion paths.

13. Close the Preview.

Student Activity: Copy and Edit a Trigger

1. Ensure that you're still working on slide 1.6 of the **CustomMenuMe3** project.

2. Duplicate a Trigger.

   ☐ on the **Triggers** panel, right-click the **Move rule 3 T Trigger** and choose **Copy**

   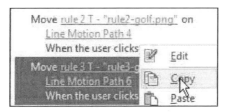

   ☐ on the **Triggers** panel, right-click the **Move rule 3 T Trigger** and choose **Paste**

   The pasted Trigger is identical to the original.

   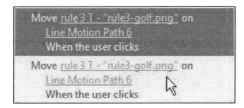

3. Edit the new Trigger.

   ☐ on the new Trigger, click the words rule **3 T - "rule3-golf-png" on Line Motion Path 6**

   ☐ from the drop-down menu, choose **rule 4 T**

   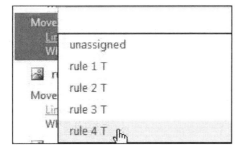

   ☐ on the new Trigger, click the words **unassigned**

   ☐ from the drop-down menu, choose **Line Motion Path 8**

   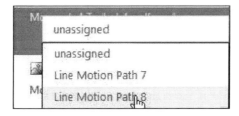

4. Preview the slide.

5. Click the Rule 2, Rule 3, and Rule 4 images.

   All three image rise as expected.

6. Click the Rule 1 image and the images reset.

7. Close the Preview.

Motion Path Resetting Confidence Check

1. Still working in the **CustomMenuMe3** project, select each of the remaining images, one at a time, and create Triggers (or copy/paste existing Triggers) that will reset the Motion Paths of the other balls when any of the balls are clicked by the learner.

   rule 2 T

   Move rule 2 T - "rule2-golf.png" on
   Line Motion Path 3
   When the user clicks

   Move rule 1 T - "rule1-golf.png" on
   Line Motion Path 2
   When the user clicks

   Move rule 3 T - "rule3-golf.png" on
   Line Motion Path 6
   When the user clicks

   Move rule 4 T - "rule4-golf.png" on
   Line Motion Path 8
   When the user clicks

   Note: You should have four Triggers for each image: one that's an odd numbered motion path that goes up; three that are even numbered motion paths that go down.

2. Preview the slide.

3. As you click each ball, the Triggers you've added should reset the position of the previously clicked images.

4. Close the Preview.

5. Save and close the project.

Student Activity: Add Triggers that Disable States

1. Open **CustomMenuMe4** from the **Storyline3_360BeyondData** folder.

2. Open slide **1.6**.

3. Preview the slide.

   As you click each of the Rule images, they rise as expected. Of course, if you click the same image again and again, it will rise and fall. However, after clicking each image, a layer is going to appear for the learners. Having the image rise and fall isn't going to make any sense when they're supposed to be reading the text in the layer. During the next few steps, you'll add a Trigger that will disable the ability to interact with an image that was just clicked.

4. Close the Preview.

5. Add a Trigger that will disable a State.

   ☐ select the **Rule 1** image

   ☐ on the **Triggers** panel, click **Create a new trigger**

   ☐ from the **Action** drop-down menu, choose **Change state of**

   ☐ from the **On Object** drop-down menu, choose **rule 1 T**

   ☐ from the **To State** drop-down menu, choose **Disabled**

   ☐ from the **When** drop-down menu, ensure **User clicks** is selected

   ☐ from the **Object** drop-down menu, ensure **rule 1 T** is selected

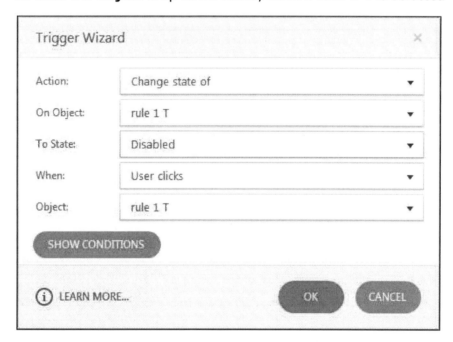

   ☐ click the **OK** button

6. Preview the slide.

7. Click the Rule 1 image and it will rise as expected. However, if you click again it won't do anything thanks to the Trigger you just created.

8. Close the Preview.

Disable States Confidence Check

1. Select the Rule **2** image and add a Trigger that disables **rule 2 T** when the User clicks.

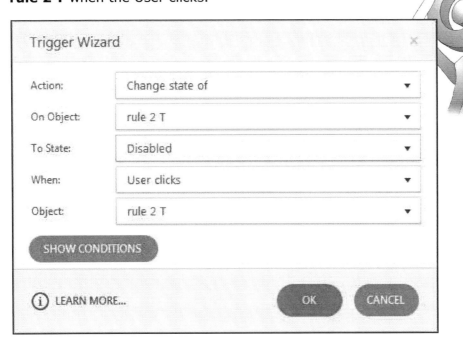

2. Repeat the same steps for Rule 3 image and then 4.

3. Preview the slide.

4. Click each of the Rule images and they rise as expected the first time they are clicked. However, if you click on any of images again they won't do anything because the Triggers you created disabled them. During the next activity, you'll learn how to re-enable states.

5. Close the Preview.

6. Close the project.

Student Activity: Add Triggers that Enable States

1. Open **CustomMenuMe5** from the **Storyline3_360BeyondData** folder.

2. Open slide **1.6**.

3. Add a Trigger that will enable a State.

   ☐ select the **Rule 1** image

   ☐ on the **Triggers** panel, click **Create a new trigger**

   ☐ from the **Action** drop-down menu, choose **Change state of**

   ☐ from the **On Object** drop-down menu, choose **rule 2 T**

   ☐ from the **To State** drop-down menu, choose **Normal**

   ☐ from the **When** drop-down menu, ensure **User clicks** is selected

   ☐ from the **Object** drop-down menu, ensure **rule 1 T** is selected

   ☐ click the **OK** button

4. Preview the slide.

5. Click the Rule **2** image and notice that it rises as expected.

6. Click the Rule **1** image and notice that it rises as expected; Rule **2** resets.

7. Try clicking the Rule **2** image again and, thanks to the Trigger you just added, notice that it is once again clickable.

8. Close the Preview.

Enable States Confidence Check

1. With the **Rule 1** image still selected, add two more Triggers (or copy/paste existing Triggers) that will **Change the state** of rules **3 T** and **4 T** to **Normal** when the User clicks.

2. Repeat the steps for Rule image 2, 3, and 4.

3. Preview the slide.

4. Click balls 2, 3, or 4. Notice that the balls rise as expected.

5. Click ball 1.

6. Now click balls 2, 3, or 4 and notice that they are clickable, thanks to the Triggers you just added.

7. Close the preview.

8. Close the project.

Triggers and Layers

If you worked through *"Articulate Storyline 3 & 360: The Essentials,"* you already know that you can create Triggers that displays a layer. In the following activity, you'll add a twist to that feature by showing a layer when the slide's Timeline begins.

Student Activity: Add a Trigger to Show a Layer

1. Open **ShowLayerMe** from the **Storyline3_360BeyondData** folder.

2. Open slide **1.6**.

3. At the bottom right of the Storyline window, notice the **Slide Layers** panel.

4. Click one time on each of the layers and observe the content on each.

5. Add a Trigger to Show a Layer when the slide opens.

   ☐ on the **Layers** panel, select the **Base Layer** (the one named **Summary**)

   ☐ on the **Triggers** panel, click **Create a new trigger**

   ☐ from the **Action** drop-down menu, choose **Show layer**

   ☐ from the **Layer** drop-down menu, choose **Base Text**

   ☐ from the **When** drop-down menu, choose **Timeline starts**

   ☐ from the **Object** drop-down menu, ensure **1.6 Summary** is selected

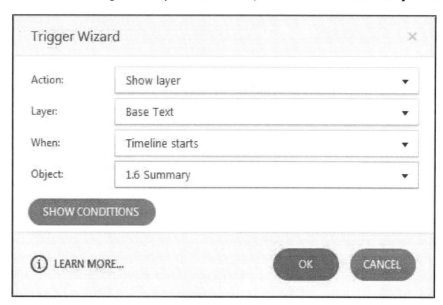

   ☐ click the **OK** button

6. Preview the slide.

   Notice that the text from the Base Text layer appears automatically.

7. Close the preview.

8. Add a Trigger to Show a Layer when an image is clicked.

   ❏ still working on slide **1.6**, select the **Rule 1** image

   ❏ on the **Triggers** panel, click **Create a new trigger**

   ❏ from the **Action** drop-down menu, choose **Show layer**

   ❏ from the **Layer** drop-down menu, choose **Rule 1 Layer**

   ❏ from the **When** drop-down menu, ensure **User clicks** is selected

   ❏ from the **Object** drop-down menu, ensure **rule 1 T** is selected

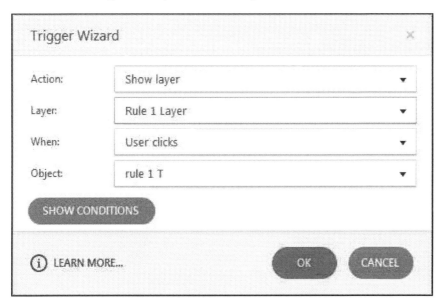

   ❏ click the **OK** button

9. Preview the slide.

10. Click the ball 1 image and notice the Rule 1 layer appears.

11. Close the preview.

Show Layers Confidence Check

1. Select each of the remaining rule images (one at a time) and add a Trigger that shows its corresponding layer when the learner clicks each ball.

Trigger Wizard		✕
Action:	Show layer	▼
Layer:	Rule 2 Layer	▼
When:	User clicks	▼
Object:	rule 2 T	▼

SHOW CONDITIONS

ⓘ LEARN MORE...   OK   CANCEL

2. Preview the slide.

3. Click the ball image to display its corresponding text.

4. Close the preview.

5. Save and close the project.

iCONLOGiC
"Skills and Drills" Learning

Module 3: Gamification

In This Module You Will Learn About:

And You Will Learn To:

Engaging the Learner with Games

An important goal of any eLearning you create is to motivate your learners and make your eLearning fun. One way to engage and motivate your learners is to add game elements into your eLearning—known as gamification. During the activities in this module, you will create a sports Jeopardy-style game that will engage your learners from the beginning to the end of the lesson.

Student Activity: Preview a Completed Project

1. Open **sports-jeopardy-finished** from the **Storyline3_360BeyondData** folder.

   Although the project consists of just a single-slide, it's fairly complex and contains sound effects, variables, Triggers and Conditional Triggers, Layers, and States.

2. Preview the project.

3. As the preview opens, notice that there is music right away. Hover your mouse above the **Continue** button and notice that there is a sound effect and hover effects.

4. Click the **Continue** button to start the lesson and notice that the music stops and a layer appears with a set of instructions.

5. Hover your mouse above the **Start** button and notice that it contains a hover state.

6. Click the **Start** button and notice that you are presented with a layer containing the game, that none of the circles on the game board are highlighted, and that your overall score is 0.

7. Click any of the circles and notice that you are presented with a question worth a specific number of points.

8. Answer the question and you'll get instant feedback in a new layer. The images you see are courtesy of the eLearning Brothers.

   As you answer the questions and move through the game board, game pieces that have been used turn red when you answer the question incorrectly and green when you answer correctly.

When you answer all of the questions, you'll see the Total Points screen with the game results.

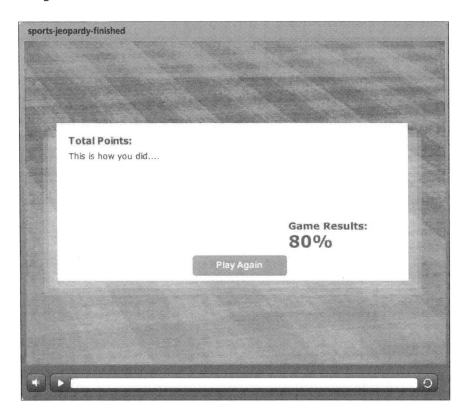

9. Close the preview.

10. Close the project.

Media and Hover States

Although it's easy to add sound to a slide, controlling when the sounds start and stop requires Triggers and Variables. In the activities that follow, you will add media to objects and use Triggers to control them. You'll learn how to use Triggers to control Hover States.

Student Activity: Start and Stop Media

1. Open **sports-jeopardy-start** from the **Storyline3_360BeyondData** folder.

2. Open the project's single slide.

3. Observe the project's existing variables.

   ❏ on the **Triggers** panel, click **Manage project variables**

The Variables dialog box opens with several variables. You learned how to create variables earlier in this book. As you move through the lessons in this module, all of the variables shown here are explained. For instance, the variable shown highlighted below (**zCategoriesGameScore**) is used on the Base Layer (it appears in the upper right of the slide as **%zCategoriesGameScore%**). This variable contains a reference to the total score earned as learners play the game.

   ❏ click the **Cancel** button

4. Add music to the slide.

- ❑ with **nothing** on the slide selected, go to the **Triggers** panel and click **Create a new trigger**
- ❑ from the **Action** drop-down menu, choose **Play media**
- ❑ from the **Media** drop-down menu, choose **Audio from File**
- ❑ from the **Storyline3_360BeyondData** folder, open **assets** folder
- ❑ from the **audio** folder, open **introMusic**
- ❑ back in the Trigger Wizard, click the **When** drop-down menu and choose **Timeline starts**
- ❑ from the **Object** drop-down menu, ensure **1.1 Categories Game** is selected

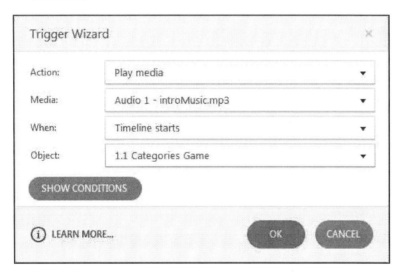

- ❑ click the **OK** button

5. Preview the project to hear the music that you just added to the slide.

6. Close the preview.

7. Add a hover and click sound effect to the **Continue** button.

- ❑ on the slide, select the **Continue** button
- ❑ on the **Triggers** panel, click **Create a new trigger**
- ❑ from the **Action** drop-down menu, choose **Play media**
- ❑ from the **Media** drop-down menu, choose **Audio from File**
- ❑ from the **Storyline3_360BeyondData** folder, open **assets** folder
- ❑ from the **audio** folder, open **gameHover**

❏ in the **Trigger Wizard**, click the **When** drop-down menu and choose **Mouse hovers over**

❏ from the **Object** drop-down menu, ensure **Continue Button** is selected

❏ click the **OK** button

8. Add an on-click sound effect to the **Continue** button.

❏ with the **Continue** button still selected, click **Create a new trigger** (on the **Triggers** panel)

❏ from the **Action** drop-down menu, choose **Play media**

❏ from the **Media** drop-down menu, choose **Audio from File**

❏ from the **Storyline3_360BeyondData** folder, open **assets** folder

❏ from the **audio** folder, open **gameClick**

❏ back in the Trigger Wizard, click the **When** drop-down menu and choose **User clicks**

❏ from the **Object** drop-down menu, ensure **Continue Button** is selected

❑ click the **OK** button

9. Preview the project to hear the music that you added originally. When you hover above the button, you'll hear a hover sound. When you click the **Continue** button, you'll hear a click sound.

10. Close the preview.

11. Show a layer.

   ❑ on the **Layers** panel, notice that the layers you need to create the game have already been created for you (you learned how to create and work with layers earlier in this book)

   ❑ ensure that you are still working on the **Base Layer (Categories Game)**

   ❑ on the slide, select the **Continue** button

   ❑ on the **Triggers** panel, click **Create a new trigger**

   ❑ from the **Action** drop-down menu, choose **Show layer**

   ❑ from the **Layer** drop-down menu, choose **Instructions**

   ❑ from the **When** drop-down menu, choose **User clicks**

   ❑ from the **Object** drop-down menu, ensure **Continue Button** is selected

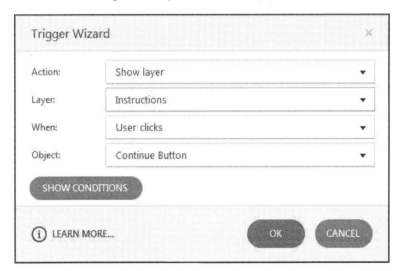

   ❑ click the **OK** button

12. Preview the project and click the **Continue** button.

   The Introduction layer appears as expected. However, the pesky background music keeps playing (it eventually fades out). You would like it to stop immediately when the **Continue** button is clicked.

13. Close the preview.

14. Create a Trigger to stop audio.

    ☐ select the **Continue** button

    ☐ on the **Triggers** panel, click **Create a new trigger**

    ☐ from the **Action** drop-down menu, choose **Stop media**

    ☐ from the **Media** drop-down menu, choose **Audio 1 - introMusic.mp3**

    ☐ from the **When** drop-down menu, choose **User clicks**

    ☐ from the **Object** drop-down menu, ensure **Continue Button** is selected

    ☐ click the **OK** button

15. Preview the project and click the **Continue** button.

    This time the music stops and the **introduction** layer appears.

16. Close the preview.

Hover and Sounds Confidence Check

1. Still working in the **sports-jeopardy-start** project, on the **Layers** panel, select the **Instructions** layer.

2. On the **Timeline**, unlock the **Start_Button** object.

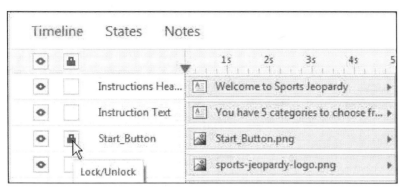

3. Create new Triggers that adds the **gameHover** and **gameClick** sound effects to the **Start Button**.

4. Preview the project and click the **Continue** button.

   The Start button should now have sounds when you hover above it and when you click it.

5. Close the preview.

6. Save and close the project.

Student Activity: Change the Hover State

1. Open **sports-jeopardy-finished** from the **Storyline3_360BeyondData** folder.

2. Preview the project and when you get to the game board, hover your mouse above the first object in the Golf column.

   Notice that there is a hover effect that has been attached to the object.

3. Click the object and answer the question correctly by choosing **B. Ty Webb**.

   Because the answer is correct, you are shown the Correct feedback layer.

4. Click the **Continue** button.

   Notice that the object you clicked now has a green border, an indication that you answered the question correctly. Also notice that when you hover over the object again, the Glow affect has been deactivated—feedback for you that you have played this part of the game already.

5. Click the **300** object in the Golf column and answer the question incorrectly by choosing **anything except C. 18**.

   Because the answer is incorrect, you are shown the Incorrect feedback layer.

6. Click the **Continue** button.

   Notice that the object you clicked now has a red border, an indication that you answered the question incorrectly. Also notice that when you hover over either the first or second object, the Glow effect has been deactivated—again, feedback for you that you have played these parts of the game already.

7. Close the preview.

8. Close the project.

9. Open **sports-jeopardy2** from the **Storyline3_360BeyondData** folder.

10. Open the project's only slide.

11. Preview the project and when you get to the game board, hover your mouse over any of the circle objects.

    Notice that as you hover over the objects, nothing happens. As you'll recall in the finished project, hovering over the objects makes the glow effect appear. You'll take care of that soon.

12. Close the preview.

13. Observe the available states.

☐ using the **Layers** panel, select the **Game Board** layer

☐ from the bottom of the Storyline window, click **States**

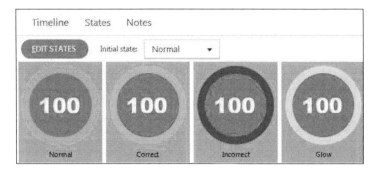

Notice that this project already contains four states: Normal, Correct, Incorrect, and **Glow**. You learned how to work with States in our *"Articulate Storyline: The Essentials"* book. You also played around with States earlier in this book (page 26). We have added these States to the current project to save you time. You'll use the States with Triggers next.

14. Create a new Trigger for an object that controls the mouse hover effect.

☐ ensure that you are on the **Game Board** layer

☐ on the **Timeline**, expand **Golf Row 100**

☐ select the **Cat 1 Row 100** object

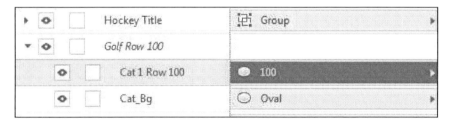

This object represents the first circle beneath the Golf category.

☐ on the **Triggers** panel, click **Create a new trigger**

☐ from the **Action** drop-down menu, choose **Change state of**

☐ from the **On Object** drop-down menu, choose **Cat 1 Row 100**

☐ from the **State** drop-down menu, choose **Glow**

Remember that Glow is one of the States already in the project.

☐ from the **When** drop-down menu, choose **Mouse hovers over**

❏ from the **Object** drop-down menu, ensure **Cat 1 Row 100** is selected

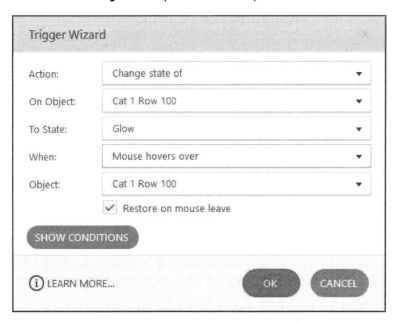

❏ click the **OK** button

15. Preview the project and when you get to the game board, hover your mouse over the first object in the Golf column.

    Notice that as you hover over the object, the object's State changes to **Glow**.

16. Close the preview.

Conditional Triggers and States

Triggers that perform a specific action are fairly cut and dry. If the learner does a specific thing, a specific action occurs. When you need a Trigger to perform actions based on a combination of events that occur in the lesson, you need Conditional Triggers.

Student Activity: Make a Trigger Conditional

1. Ensure **sports-jeopardy2** is still open.

2. Observe the Properties of an existing variable.

   ❏ on the **Triggers** panel, click **Manage project variables**

   The Variables dialog box opens.

   ❏ select **zCategoriesStateC1Q100**

   This Text variable has a Default Value of **normal**. You are going to use this default variable as a condition to allow the hover state to appear. Later, you will change the value from **normal** to **incorrect** or **correct**.

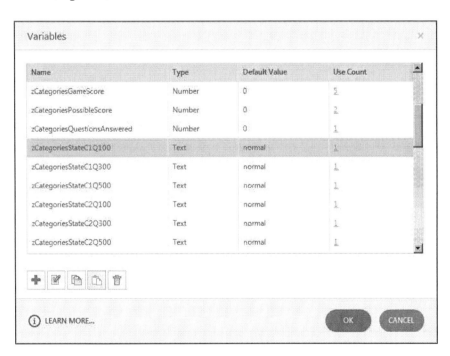

   ❏ click the **Cancel** button

3. Make the Hover State Conditional.

   ❏ on the **Triggers** panel, double-click **Change state of Cat 1 Row 100**

   The Trigger Wizard opens.

   ❏ from the bottom of the dialog box, click **Show Conditions**
   ❏ click the **plus sign** to add a condition

☐ from the **If** drop-down menu, choose **zCategoriesStateC1Q100**

☐ from the **Operator** drop-down menu, choose **== Equal to**

☐ from the **Type** drop-down menu, ensure **Value** is selected

☐ in the **Value** field, type **normal**

☐ click the **OK** button

☐ click the **OK** button

Effects Confidence Check

1. Still working in the **sports-jeopardy2** project, add the Hover effect Trigger to both the 300 and 500 objects in the Golf column.

2. Ensure that both new Triggers are Conditional if **zCategoriesStateC1Q300** and then **zCategoriesStateC1Q500** are **Equal** to **normal**.

3. Preview the project.

   You are able to test the Hover effect but not the condition. You will be able to test that soon.

4. Close the preview.

5. Save and close the project.

Student Activity: Show Layers Conditionally

1. Open **sports-jeopardy3** from the **Storyline3_360BeyondData** folder.

2. Show a layer conditionally.

   ❑ ensure that you are on the **Game Board** layer
   ❑ on the **Timeline**, expand **Golf Row 100**
   ❑ select the **Cat 1 Row 100** object
   ❑ on the **Triggers** panel, click **Create a new trigger**
   ❑ from the **Action** drop-down menu, choose **Show layer**

   There are several layers. Each question on the board has three associated layers. A question layer with possible answer, a Correct layer, and an Incorrect layer. You will create a Trigger that displays the Question 100 layer if the state of the 100 is normal.

   ❑ from the **Layer** drop-down menu, choose **Category 1 - Question 100**
   ❑ from the **When** drop-down menu, choose **User clicks**
   ❑ from the **Object** drop-down menu, choose **Cat 1 Row 100**

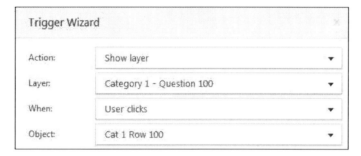

   ❑ from the bottom of the dialog box, click **Show Conditions**
   ❑ click the **plus sign** to add a condition
   ❑ from the **If** drop-down menu, choose **zCategoriesStateC1Q100**
   ❑ from the **Operator** drop-down menu, choose **== Equal to**
   ❑ from the **Type** drop-down menu, ensure **Value** is selected
   ❑ in the **Value** field, type **normal**

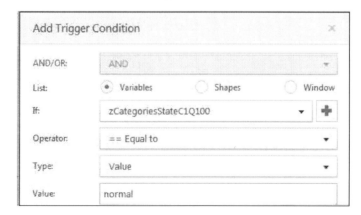

❑ click the **OK** button twice (to close both dialog boxes)

3. Preview the project and once the game board appears, click the 100 beneath golf.

   The question layer appears.

4. Close the preview.

Conditions Confidence Check

1. Still working in the **sports-jeopardy3** project, add the Triggers necessary to show the **Category 1 - Question 300** layer and then the **Category 1 - Question 500** layer.

2. Ensure that both new Triggers are Conditional if **zCategoriesStateC1Q300** and then **zCategoriesStateC1Q500** are **Equal** to **normal**.

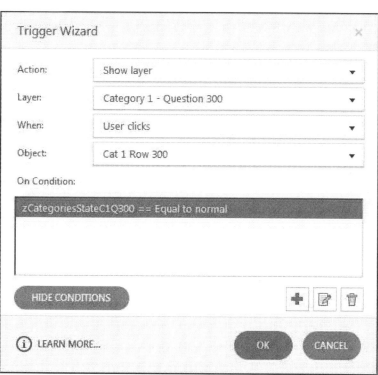

3. Preview the project. You should be able to click on the **100**, **300**, or **500** in the **Golf** column and see the related question layer.

4. Close the preview.

5. Save and close the project.

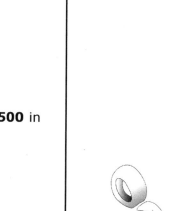

Student Activity: Hide Objects Using States

1. Open **sports-jeopardy4** from the **Storyline3_360BeyondData** folder.

2. Open the project's only slide.

3. Observe the project's existing layers.

   ☐ on the **Slide Layers** panel, notice that there are several layers.

   ☐ select the **Category 1 - Question 100** layer

   This layer contains the question and possible answers. Just above the Category 1 - Question 100 layer, there are two layers called **Category 1 - Question 100 - Incorrect** and **Category 1 - Question 100 - Correct**. In the steps that follow, you're going to create a Trigger that hides the answers on the **Category 1 - Question 100** layer and displays one of the other layers (depending upon what the learner clicks).

4. Add a Trigger to show correct or incorrect layers.

   ☐ on the Slide Layers panel, ensure the **Category 1 - Question 100** layer is selected

   ☐ on the layer, select **A. Fletch**

   This is one of the incorrect answers.

   ☐ on the **Triggers** panel, click **Create a new trigger**

   ☐ from the **Action** drop-down menu, choose **Show layer**

   ☐ from the **Layer** drop-down menu, choose **Category 1 - Question 100-Incorrect**

   ☐ from the **When** drop-down menu, choose **User clicks**

   ☐ from the **Object** drop-down menu, ensure **Option 1** is selected

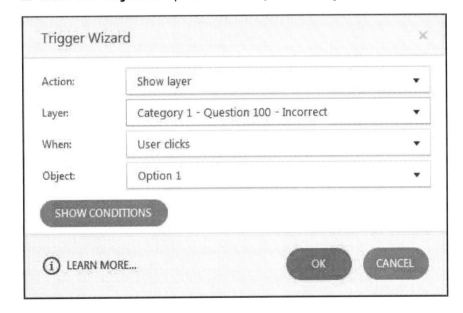

   ☐ click the **OK** button

- ☐ on the Slide Layers panel, ensure the **Category 1 - Question 100** layer is selected
- ☐ on the layer, select **B. Ty Webb**

This is the correct answer.

- ☐ on the **Triggers** panel, click **Create a new trigger**
- ☐ from the **Action** drop-down menu, choose **Show layer**
- ☐ from the **Layer** drop-down menu, choose **Category 1 - Correct**
- ☐ from the **When** drop-down menu, choose **User clicks**
- ☐ from the **Object** drop-down menu, ensure **Option 2** is selected

Trigger Wizard	✕
Action:	Show layer ▼
Layer:	Category 1 - Question 100 - Correct ▼
When:	User clicks ▼
Object:	Option 2 ▼

SHOW CONDITIONS

ⓘ LEARN MORE...   OK   CANCEL

- ☐ click the **OK** button
- ☐ on the layer, select **C. Clark**

This is another incorrect answer.

- ☐ on the **Triggers** panel, click **Create a new trigger**
- ☐ from the **Action** drop-down menu, choose **Show layer**
- ☐ from the **Layer** drop-down menu, choose **Category 1 - Incorrect**
- ☐ from the **When** drop-down menu, choose **User clicks**

❑ from the **Object** drop-down menu, ensure **Option 3** is selected

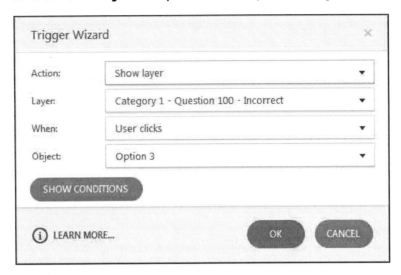

❑ click the **OK** button

❑ on the layer, select **D. Oswald**

This is the last incorrect answer.

❑ on the **Triggers** panel, click **Create a new trigger**

❑ from the **Action** drop-down menu, choose **Show layer**

❑ from the **Layer** drop-down menu, choose **Category 1 - Incorrect**

❑ from the **When** drop-down menu, choose **User clicks**

❑ from the **Object** drop-down menu, ensure **Option 4** is selected

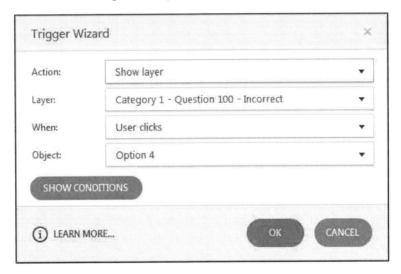

❑ click the **OK** button

5. Preview the project until you get to the game board.

6. From below the Golf category, click **100**.

When you select a wrong answer, you'll see the layer containing the "incorrect" or "correct" message. However, when you look to the left or the right of the feedback message, you'll see that part of the answers are still visible. You need these objects to "hide" as learners answer the question. You'll take care of that next.

7. Close the preview.

8. Hide objects using States.

   ❑ on the **Slide Layers** panel, ensure that the **Category 1 - Question 100** layer is still selected

   ❑ on the layer, select **A. Fletch**

   ❑ on the **Triggers** panel, click **Create a new trigger**

   ❑ from the **Action** drop-down menu, choose **Change state of**

   ❑ from the **On Object** drop-down menu, choose **Option 1**

   ❑ from the **To State** drop-down menu, choose **Hidden**

   ❑ from the **When** drop-down menu, choose **User clicks**

   ❑ from the **Object** drop-down menu, ensure **Option 1** is selected

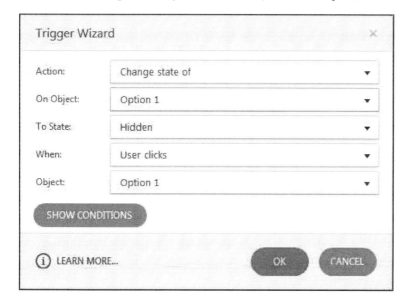

   ❑ click the **OK** button

☐ on the layer, ensure **Fletch** is still selected

☐ on the **Triggers** panel, click **Create a new trigger**

☐ from the **Action** drop-down menu, choose **Change state of**

☐ from the **On Object** drop-down menu, choose **Option 2**

☐ from the **To State** drop-down menu, choose **Hidden**

☐ from the **When** drop-down menu, ensure **User clicks** is selected

☐ from the **Object** drop-down menu, ensure **Option 1** is selected

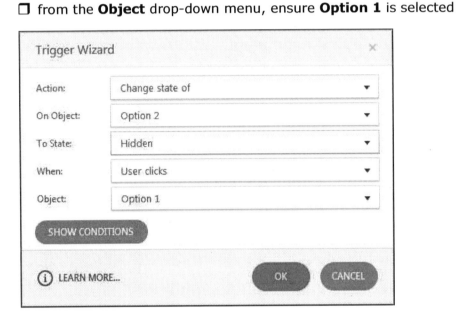

☐ click the **OK** button

Show Layers Confidence Check

1. Still working in the **sports-jeopardy4** project, add two more Triggers to the **Fletch** object that changes the State of **Option 3** and **Option 4** to **Hidden** when the **User clicks**.

2. Preview the project and, from below the Golf category, click **100**.

   After answering the question this time, the answers disappear when the feedback text appears.

3. Close the preview.

4. Save and close the project.

Student Activity: Adjust a Variable

1. Open **sports-jeopardy5** from the **Storyline3_360BeyondData** folder.

2. Open the project's only slide.

3. Adjust a Variable to set the value of each question to "correct" or "incorrect" based on the answer a learner chooses.

   ☐ on the **Slide Layers** panel, select the **Category 1 - Question 100 - Correct** layer

   ☐ on the layer, select the **Continue** button

   ☐ on the **Triggers** panel, click **Create a new trigger**

   ☐ from the **Action** drop-down menu, choose **Adjust variable**

   ☐ from the **Variable** drop-down menu, choose **zCategoriesStateC1Q100**

   ☐ from the **Operator** drop-down menu, choose **= Assignment**

   ☐ from the **Value** drop-down menu, choose **Value**

   ☐ in the next field, type **correct**

   ☐ from the **When** drop-down menu, choose **User clicks**

   ☐ from the **Object** drop-down menu, ensure **Continue** is selected

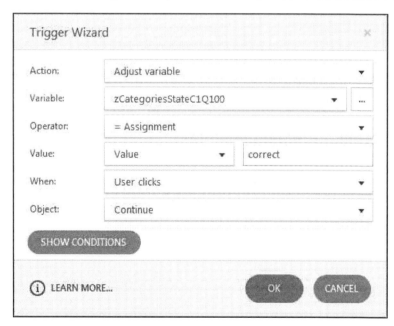

   ☐ click the **OK** button

4. Show a layer.

   ☐ on the **Triggers** panel, click **Create a new trigger**

   ☐ from the **Action** drop-down menu, choose **Show layer**

   ☐ from the **Layer** drop-down menu, choose **Game Board**

   ☐ from the **When** drop-down menu, choose **User clicks**

❒ from the **Object** drop-down menu, ensure **Continue** is selected

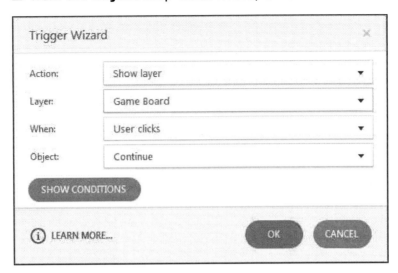

❒ click the **OK** button

5. Preview the project and from below the **Golf** category, click **100**.

After answering the question correctly or incorrectly, the answers disappear when the feedback text appears.

6. Close the preview.

7. Save the project.

Student Activity: Change a State Based on When

1. Ensure that the **sports-jeopardy5** project is still open.

   In the steps that follow you will make the appearance of the question circle in the game board change based on whether a question was answered correctly or incorrectly.

2. Change the State of an object when the Timeline starts.

   ☐ on the **Slide Layers** panel, select the **Game Board** layer

   ☐ with nothing on the layer selected, **create a new Trigger**

   ☐ from the **Action** drop-down menu, choose **Change state of**

   ☐ from the **On Object** drop-down menu, choose **Cat 1 Row 100**

   ☐ from the **To State** drop-down menu, choose **Correct**

   ☐ from the **When** drop-down menu, ensure **Timeline starts** is selected

   ☐ from the **Object** drop-down menu, ensure **Game Board** is selected

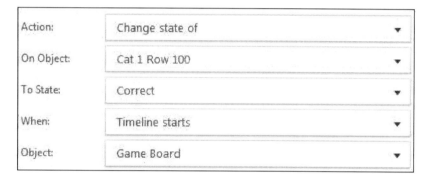

   ☐ from the bottom of the dialog box, click **Show Conditions**

   ☐ from the bottom right of the dialog box, click **Add a new "AND" or "OR" condition**

   ☐ from the **If** drop-down menu, choose **zCategoriesStateC1Q100**

   ☐ from the **Operator** drop-down menu, choose **== Equal to**

   ☐ from the **Type** drop-down menu, ensure **Value** is selected

   ☐ in the **Value** field, type **correct**

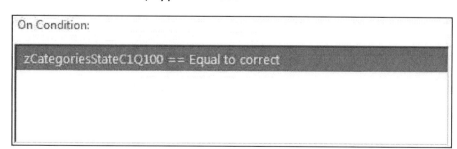

   ☐ click the **OK** button twice to close both dialog boxes

3. Preview the project and from below the **Golf** category, click **100**.

4. Answer the question correctly (B. Ty Webb) and then click the **Continue** button.

   Notice that the State of the 100 has changed to green indicating you answered the question correctly.

5. Close the preview.

Show Layers Confidence Check

1. Still working in the **sports-jeopardy5** project, select the **Category 1 - Question 100 - Incorrect** layer.

2. Add a Trigger to the **Continue** button that adjusts the Variable **zCategoriesStateC1Q100** to a Value of **incorrect**.

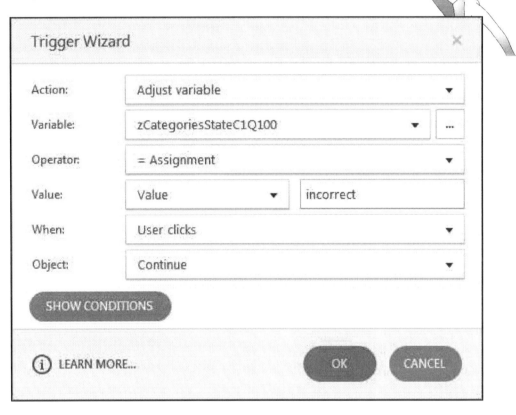

3. Add another Trigger to the **Continue** button that shows the layer called Game Board When the User clicks.

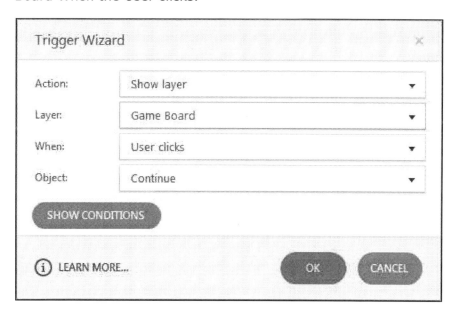

4. Select the **Game Board** layer and with nothing selected, create a new Trigger that changes the State of **Cat 1 Row 100** to **Incorrect** when the Timeline Starts. Add the Condition **If zCategoriesStateC1Q100** that uses the Operator **== Equal to**. Set the Type to **Value** and the Value to **incorrect**.

5. Preview the project and, after arriving at the game board, from below the **Golf** category, click **100**.

6. Answer the question incorrectly (select anything except B. Ty Webb) and then click the **Continue** button.

    The state of the 100 should change to red indicating that you answered the question incorrectly.

7. Close the preview.

8. Save and close the project.

Student Activity: Calculate a Score

1. Open **sports-jeopardy6** from the **Storyline3_360BeyondData** folder.

2. Open the project's only slide.

   At the top of the slide there is a reference to a variable that has already been added to the project (**zCategoriesGameScore**). Its default value is **0**. As learners access the lesson and play the game, their score will adjust automatically. During the following steps, you're going to adjust the variable so that it calculates an appropriate score depending upon how many correct answers are selected by the learner.

3. Increment a variable by 100.

   ☐ on the **Slide Layers** panel, select **Category 1 - Question 100 Correct**

   ☐ using the **Triggers** panel, create a **New Trigger**

   ☐ from the **Action** drop-down menu, choose **Adjust variable**

   ☐ from the **Variable** drop-down menu, choose **zCategoriesGameScore**

   ☐ from the **Value** drop-down menu, choose **Value**

   ☐ from the **Operator** drop-down menu, ensure that **+ Add** is selected

   ☐ type **100** into the field beside **Value**

   ☐ from the **When** drop-down menu, choose **Timeline starts**

   ☐ from the **Object** drop-down menu, ensure **Category 1 - Question 100 Correct** is selected

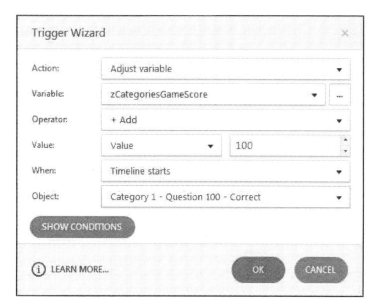

□ click the **OK** button

4. Preview the project and after arriving at the game board, notice that the score is currently 0.

5. From below the **Golf** category, click **100**.

6. Answer the question correctly (choose B. Ty Webb). Notice that the score increases from 0 to 100.

7. Click the **Continue** button.

8. Close the preview.

Calculating Confidence Check

1. Still working in the **sports-jeopardy6** project, select the **Category 1 - Question 300 - Correct** layer.

2. Add a new Trigger that adjusts the value of the **zCategoriesGameScore** variable by 300.

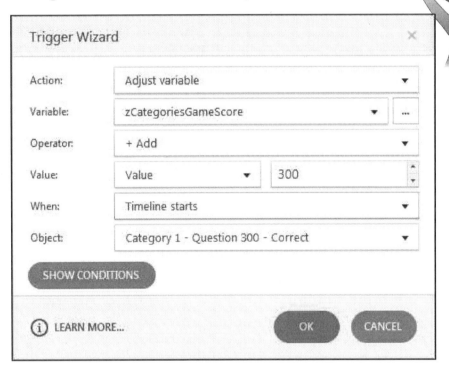

3. Select the **Category 1 - Question 500 - Correct** layer.

4. Add a new Trigger that adjusts the value of the **zCategoriesGameScore** variable by 500.

5. Preview the project and after arriving at the game board, answer all three of the **Golf** questions. If you answer all of the questions correctly, you should receive a score of 900.

6. Close the preview.

7. Save and close the project.

Student Activity: Adjust Variables Dynamically

1. Open **sports-jeopardy7** from the **Storyline3_360BeyondData** folder.

2. Open the project's only slide.

3. Observe the existing Variables.

   ❑ on the **Triggers** panel, click **Manage Project Variables**

   There are two variables of note in the Variables dialog box. One is called **zCategoriesPossibleScore**. This variable has a Default Value of 0, which will store the total value of the score the learner gets if they answer every question in the game correctly. The second is called **zCategoriesGameScorePercentage**. This variable also has a Default Value of 0. Its score will be adjusted dynamically to show the percentage of total points earned by the learner (in relationship to the total possible score of 4500) as they play the game.

zCategoriesGameScorePercentage	Number	0
zCategoriesPossibleScore	Number	0

   ❑ click the **Cancel** button

4. Observe a variable reference on a layer.

   ❑ on the **Slide Layers** panel, select the **Game Board** layer

   At the top of the layer notice that there is a reference to the **zCategoriesGameScorePercentage** Variable. As points are earned, the percentage of points earned appears here.

5. Create a Trigger that sets the value of a Variable to match another.

   ❑ ensure that you're working on the **Game Board** layer and that nothing is selected

   ❑ using the **Triggers** panel, create a **New Trigger**

   ❑ from the **Action** drop-down menu, choose **Adjust variable**

   ❑ from the **Variable** drop-down menu, choose **zCategoriesGameScorePercentage**

   ❑ from the **Operator** drop-down menu, choose **= Assignment**

   ❑ from the **Value** drop-down menu, choose **Variable**

   ❑ from the next drop-down menu, choose **zCategoriesGameScore**

   ❑ from the **When** drop-down menu, choose **Timeline starts**

☐ from the **Object** drop-down menu, ensure **Game Board** is selected

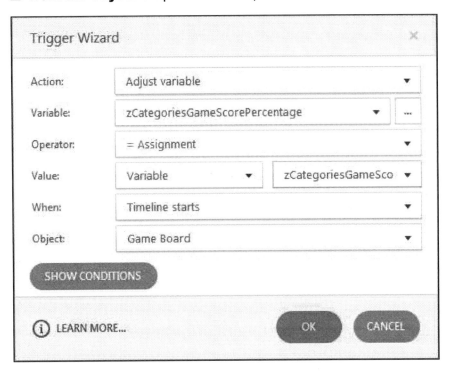

☐ click the **OK** button

6. Create a Trigger that shows results as a fraction.

☐ ensure that you're working on the **Game Board** layer and that nothing is selected

☐ using the **Triggers** panel, create a **New Trigger**

☐ from the **Action** drop-down menu, choose **Adjust variable**

☐ from the **Variable** drop-down menu, choose **zCategoriesGameScorePercentage**

☐ from the **Operator** drop-down menu, choose **/ Divide**

☐ from the **Value** drop-down menu, choose **Variable**

☐ from the next drop-down menu, choose **zCategoriesPossibleScore**

☐ from the **When** drop-down menu, choose **Timeline starts**

❏ from the **Object** drop-down menu, ensure **Game Board** is selected

❏ click the **OK** button

7. Create a Trigger that shows results as a percentage.

❏ ensure that you're working on the **Game Board** layer and that nothing is selected

❏ using the **Triggers** panel, create a **New Trigger**

❏ from the **Action** drop-down menu, choose **Adjust variable**

❏ from the **Variable** drop-down menu, choose **zCategoriesGameScorePercentage**

❏ from the **Operator** drop-down menu, choose *** Multiply**

❏ from the **Value** drop-down menu, choose **Value**

❏ from the next field, type **100**

❏ from the **When** drop-down menu, choose **Timeline starts**

❏ from the **Object** drop-down menu, ensure **Game Board** is selected

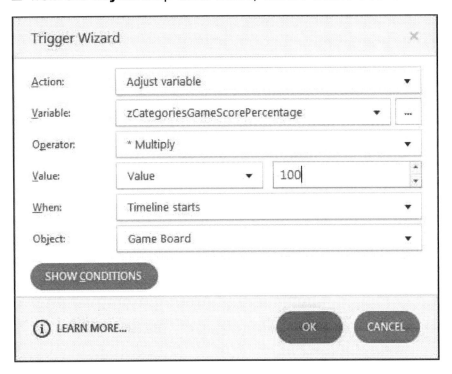

❏ click the **OK** button

8. Preview the project and after arriving at the game board, notice that the score is **0** and the percentage is **0%**.

9. Play the game and answer questions as you see fit. If you get some of the answers correct, you'll see two things. First, the score increases. Second, the percentage of your possible score is automatically calculated and displayed.

10. Close the preview.

11. Close the project.

Module 4: Video Control and Sliders

In This Module You Will Learn About:

- Advanced Video Control, page 100
- Cue Points, page 105
- Sliders, page 111

And You Will Learn To:

- Work with Web Objects, page 100
- Edit Video Parameters, page 103
- Add Cue Points to the Timeline, page 105
- Add Triggers Based on Cue Points, page 107
- Change a Character's State Based on Time, page 109
- Insert and Format a Slider, page 111
- Set Slider Values, page 113
- Add Triggers to a Slider, page 114

Advanced Video Control

You learned how to insert a video into a Storyline project in *"Articulate Storyline: The Essentials."* But there's more to video than simply inserting it and allowing it to automatically play. During the first part of this module, you will learn how to insert YouTube Videos (or videos from other video streaming services such as Vimeo), and how to control the playback of a video.

Student Activity: Work with Web Objects

1. Open **VideoMe** from the **Storyline3_360BeyondData** folder.

2. Open slide **1.5**.

3. Insert a Web Object.

   ☐ click the **Insert** tab on the Ribbon and, from the **Media** group, click **Web Object**

   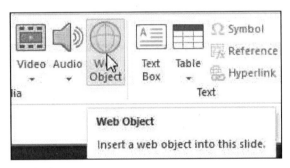

   The Insert Web Object dialog box opens.

   ☐ in the **Enter a web address** field, type **http://www.youtube.com/ embed/ACsALN7Y7T8**

   Note: Because typos can result in a failed link, check the text that you typed carefully. If typing is not your thing, we've added the web address to the **Notes** panel. (You'll find that panel at the bottom of the Storyline window next to Timeline and States. You can copy/paste the web address instead of typing it.)

   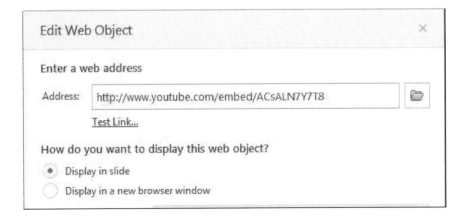

You were instructed to type the word "embed" into the web address. Why? There are two ways to add videos into your eLearning lesson. One is called **iFrame**; the other is called **embed**. Using iFrame, you can control video parameters such as player controls, video title, and player actions. Unfortunately, you cannot test iFrame videos without first publishing a project to a web server or an LMS. From a development standpoint, embedding videos is a better option because you can preview your work at any time. The "ACsALN7Y7T8" text is the ID associated with a specific YouTube video. Once any video is posted to YouTube, it is assigned a unique ID.

❏ click the **OK** button

4. Resize the web object until your slide is similar to the image below.

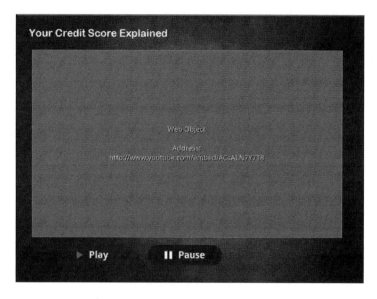

5. Publish the project as HTML5 only.

❏ choose **File > Publish**

❏ from the categories at the left, click **Web**

❏ to the right of Folder, click **Browse** and open **Storyline3_360BeyondData > published_projects**

❏ click the **link** in **Formats** area and drag the slider to **HTML5**

❏ click the **OK** button

❏ click the red **Publish** button

❏ after the project is published, click the **View Project** button

❏ from the Menu at the left, click **Your Credit Score Explained**

❏ from the middle of the screen, click the **Play** button

The video plays directly in the Web Object. Fast forward to the end of the video. When the video ends, you see related videos. Although related videos are can be helpful, you'll sometimes see inappropriate content. Next you will edit the parameters of the embedded video and remove the related videos.

6. Close the browser and return to the Storyline project

7. Close the **Publish Successful** dialog box.

Student Activity: Edit Video Parameters

1. Ensure that the **VideoMe** project is still open and you're working on slide 1.5.

2. Edit video parameters.

   ❏ select the Web Object on the slide

   ❏ from the **Web Object Tools** tab on the Ribbon, click **Edit**

   The **Edit Web Object** dialog box opens.

   ❏ in the **Enter a web address** field, add the following text at the end of the current web address: **?rel=0**

   A question mark tells Storyline that you want to add a parameter. The "rel" is the related video parameter. Setting the value to "0" disables the related videos.

   ❏ click the **OK** button

3. Publish the project as HTML5 again.

4. View the project.

5. From the Menu at the left, click **Your Credit Score Explained** again and play the video.

6. Fast forward to the end of the video and notice that there are no longer any related videos.

7. Close the browser and return to the Storyline project

8. Close the **Publish Successful** dialog box.

Parameters Confidence Check

You'll now get a chance to add your own video parameters to the embedded video. Here are two common video parameters:

autoplay: The autoplay parameter determines whether the video automatically plays when learners reach the slide that contains the YouTube web object or whether learners must click the video to start playing it. The autoplay parameter accepts the following values: **0** means you do not want the video to autoplay (default); **1** means you want the video to autoplay.

cc_load_policy: The cc_load_policy parameter determines whether closed captions are displayed by default in the YouTube video. The cc_load_policy parameter accepts the following value: **1** means you want existing closed captions to be displayed by default.

Note: The cc_load_policy parameter displays only existing captions in the YouTube video. You must first add captions to the video through your account at http://YouTube.com. You can add captions only to videos you own. (If you don't own the video you're embedding, the cc_load_policy parameter will display captions only if the owner has already added them to the YouTube video.)

1. Open the **Edit Web Object** dialog box and add an ampersand (**&**) after the parameter you added a moment ago.

2. Add the **autoplay** parameter so that the video automatically plays.

3. Add another ampersand and then add the **cc_load_policy** parameter.

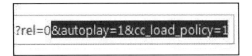

4. Publish the project and click **Your Credit Score Explained**.

   This time, the video should automatically play and you'll see closed captions that were added by the video owner.

   Note: You can see more official parameters by visiting: https://developers.google.com/youtube/player_parameters?hl=en#Parameters.

Cue Points

A Cue Point is a marker that can be used to precisely align objects on the Timeline. In addition, Cue Points can be used to activate Triggers based on a Cue Point's position on the Timeline. There are multiple ways to add Cue Points. You can right-click on the Timeline or press the [**c**] key on your keyboard.

In the activity that follows, you will add five Cue Points to a project. The position of those Cue Points will be used to Trigger the appearance of layers.

Student Activity: Add Cue Points to the Timeline

1. Open **VideoTimeMe** from the **Storyline3_360BeyondData** folder.

2. Open side **1.5**.

3. Add a Cue Point to the Timeline.

   ☐ on the **Timeline**, scroll right until you can see the **35 second mark**

   ☐ on the **Timeline**, click the number **35s**

   Notice that the Playhead moves to 35s. At this point in the video, the narrator is discussing payment history as it relates to a credit score. You are going to have a layer called **payment history** (it has text and an image that supports the video) appear at this point in time.

   ☐ right-click anywhere on the Timeline and choose **Create Cue Point at Playhead**

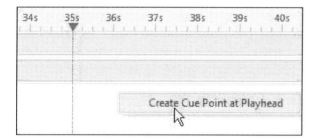

The Cue Point appears on the Timeline at 35s.

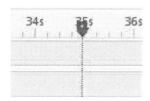

Note: If you are having trouble positioning the Playhead exactly where you want it along the Timeline, try pressing [**shift**] while dragging the Playhead (the Playhead should snap to tick marks along the Timeline).

4. Add a Cue Point with the keyboard.

   ☐ on the **Timeline**, position the Playhead at the **99s** mark

   You are going to have a layer called **amount owed** appear at this point.

   ☐ on your keyboard, press [**c**]

Cue Points Confidence Check

1. Add additional Cue Points along the Timeline at Playhead positions:

   178s

   230s

   257s

   The project should now have five Cue Points.

2. Save your work.

Student Activity: Add Triggers Based on Cue Points

1. Ensure that the **VideoTimeMe** project is still open.

2. On the **Slide Layers** panel, notice that there are several layers in the project.

3. Explore some of the layers.

   ☐ on the **Slide Layers** panel, click any of the layers except for the **Base Layer**

   Each layer, such as **payment history layer**, contains a character with two States. One State shows the character in a normal pose; the other shows the character holding up different fingers.

4. Select the **Base Layer** (Your Credit Score Explained).

5. Create a Trigger that shows a layer based on a Cue Point.

   ☐ on the **Triggers** panel, create a new Trigger

   The Trigger Wizard dialog box opens.

   ☐ from the **Action** drop-down menu, choose **Show layer**
   ☐ from the **Layer** drop-down menu, choose **payment history layer**
   ☐ from the **When** drop-down menu, choose **Timeline reaches**
   ☐ from the **Time** drop-down menu, choose **Cue point**
   ☐ from the next drop-down menu, choose **#1 (35s)**

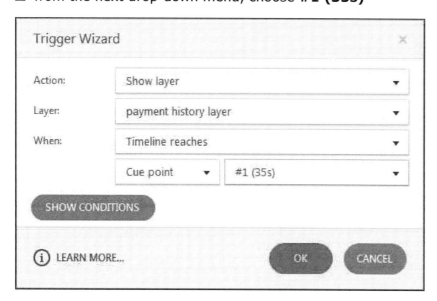

   ☐ click the **OK** button

Triggers and Cue Points Confidence Check

1. Create four more Triggers that **Show layers** based on **Cue Points**.

   Trigger 2: Shows the **amount owed layer** at Cue point **#2**.

   Trigger 3: Shows the **length of credit layer** at Cue point **#3**.

   Trigger 4: Shows the **new credit layer** at Cue point **#4**.

   Trigger 5: Shows the **type of credit layer** at Cue point **#5**.

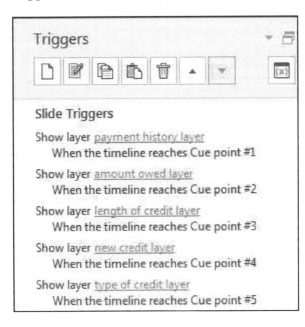

2. Preview the slide.

   Keep in mind that while you are previewing, the video web object will not play. However, you will see the layers appear with the character as each Cue Point is reached.

3. Close the preview and save your work.

Student Activity: Change a Character's State Based on Time

1. Ensure that the **VideoTimeMe** project is still open.

2. On the Slide Layers panel, select the **payment history layer**.

3. Change a Character's State based on time.

   ❏ on the **Triggers** panel, create a new Trigger

   The Trigger Wizard dialog box opens.

   ❏ from the **Action** drop-down menu, choose **Change state of**

   ❏ from the **On Object** drop-down menu, choose **Character 1**

   ❏ from the **To State** drop-down menu, choose **1 finger**

   ❏ from the **When** drop-down menu, choose **Timeline reaches**

   ❏ in the **Time** field to the right of Time, type **2**

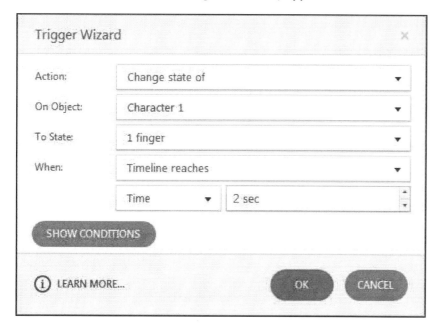

   ❏ click the **OK** button

4. Preview the slide.

   Pay attention to the layer that appears at 35 seconds. Two seconds after it appears, the character holds up a single finger.

5. Close the preview and save your work.

States Based on Time Confidence Check

1. Still working on the payment history layer, right-click the Trigger you just created and choose **Copy.**

2. On the Layers panel, select the **amount owed layer**.

3. On the Triggers panel, right-click and choose **Paste** (to add the copied Trigger from the Clipboard to the Triggers panel).

4. On the Triggers panel, double-click the pasted Trigger to open the Trigger Wizard.

5. From the **On Object** drop-down menu, choose **Character 1**.

6. Notice that because this is a copy of an existing Trigger, the **When** is already set.

7. Paste the Trigger on the **length of credit layer**.

8. Edit the Trigger by changing the On Object to **Character 1**.

9. Paste the Trigger on the **new credit layer**.

10. Edit the Trigger by changing the **On Object** to **Character 1**.

11. Paste the Trigger on the **type of credit layer**.

12. Edit the Trigger by changing the **On Object** to **Character 1**.

13. Preview the slide.

    As the layers appear, notice that the character raises different fingers. (**Note:** The video is a bit long; you can drag the seek bar to the right to view the layers and save some time.)

14. Close the preview, save your work, and then close the project.

Sliders

Sliders are interactive objects that allow a Storyline developer to manipulate objects, control data, or affect object States. In the activities that follow, you will create a slider that changes the appearance of a bar chart as a learner drags the slider.

Student Activity: Insert and Format a Slider

1. Preview a finished Slider.

   ❏ open **SliderMeFinished** from the **Storyline3_360BeyondData** folder

2. Open slide **1.4**.

3. Preview the slide.

   The Slider is the bar that you see on the bottom of the slide.

4. On the Slider, drag the green pointer **left or right**. As you do, notice that the State of the green rectangle changes. You will be creating this Slider during the activities that follow.

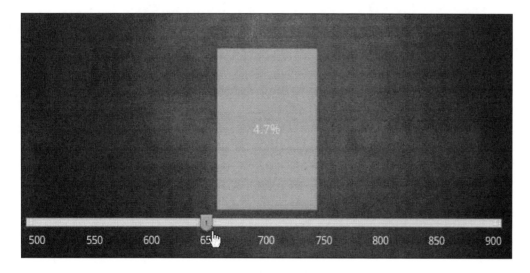

5. Close the preview and then close the project.

6. Open **SliderMe** from the **Storyline3_360BeyondData** folder.

7. Open slide **1.4**.

8. Select the green rectangle on the slide.

9. Select **States**.

   Notice that the project already contains multiple States for the rectangle.

10. Insert a Slider.

☐ select the **Insert** tab on the Ribbon

☐ from the **Interactive Objects** group, click **Slider**

☐ select the **first slider**

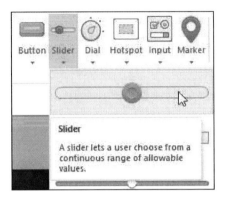

☐ on the slide, draw and position a Slider similar to the image below

There are two parts to a Slider: the **Thumb** (the circle) and the **Track** (the bar).

11. Change the styles of the Thumb and the Track.

☐ ensure that the **Slider is selected**

☐ on the Ribbon, **Slider Tools** tab, **Format**, go to the **Thumb Styles** menu at the left and choose **any Thumb Style**

☐ on the Ribbon, **Slider Tools Format** tab, go to the **Track Styles** menu and choose any **Track Style**

Student Activity: Set Slider Values

1. Ensure that the **SliderMe** project is still open, and that you are still working on slide **1.4**.

2. Set the Slider's Start and End values.

   ❏ with the Slider selected, select the Slider Tools **Design** tab

   ❏ change the Start to **500**

   ❏ change the End to **900**

   The Start and End options now match the numbers that were already on the slide (beneath the Slider).

3. Set the Slider's Initial value.

   ❏ with the Slider selected, change the **Initial** value to **700**

   On the Slider, notice that the Thumb is now positioned in the middle (at 700).

4. Set the Step value.

   ❏ with the Slider selected, change the **Step** value to **50**

   When the learner drags the Thumb, it will jump in increments of 50.

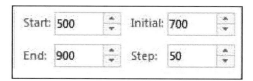

Student Activity: Add Triggers to a Slider

1. Ensure that the **SliderMe** project is still open and you are still working on slide **1.4**.

2. Add a Trigger to the Slider.

   ❏ ensure that the Slider is selected

   ❏ on the **Triggers** panel, click **Manage project variables**

   The Variables dialog box opens. At the bottom of the list, the Slider1 variable was automatically created by Storyline when you inserted the Slider. In addition, the **Default Value** of 700 was set when you set the **Initial Value** a moment ago.

| Slider1 | Number | 700 |

   ❏ click the **Cancel** button

   ❏ on the **Triggers** panel, create a new Trigger

   ❏ from the **Action** drop-down menu, choose **Change state of**

   ❏ from the **On Object** drop-down menu, choose **Rate Rectangle**

   ❏ from the **To State** drop-down menu, choose **750**

   ❏ from the **When** drop-down menu, choose **Slider moves**

   ❏ from the **Slider** drop-down menu, choose **Slider 1**

   ❏ from the **Condition** drop-down menu, choose **== Equal to**

   ❏ in the next field, type **750**

   ❏ click the **OK** button

3. Preview the slide.

4. On the Slider, drag the Thumb to **750**. Notice that the State of the green rectangle changes.

5. Close the preview and save your work.

Sliders Confidence Check

1. Copy and paste the Trigger you just created.

2. Edit the newest Trigger (change its **To State** to **800** and the **Condition value** to **800**).

3. Copy and paste the newest Trigger.

4. Edit the newest Trigger (change its **To State** to **850** and the **Condition value** to **850**).

5. Copy and paste the newest Trigger.

6. Edit the newest Trigger (change its **To State** to **900** and the **Condition value** to **900**).

7. Copy and paste the newest Trigger.

8. Edit the newest Trigger (change its **To State** to **Normal** and the **Condition value** to **700**).

9. Copy and paste the newest Trigger.

10. Edit the newest Trigger (change its **To State** to **650** and the **Condition value** to **650**).

11. Copy and paste the newest Trigger.

12. Edit the newest Trigger (change its **To State** to **600** and the **Condition value** to **600**).

13. Copy and paste the newest Trigger.

14. Edit the newest Trigger (change its **To State** to **550** and the **Condition value** to **550**).

15. Copy and paste the newest Trigger.

16. Edit the newest Trigger (change its **To State** to **500** and the **Condition value** to **500**).

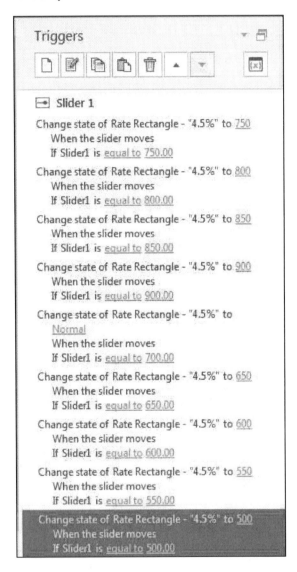

17. Preview the slide.

18. On the Slider, drag the Thumb to the **left or right**. As you do, notice that the State of the green rectangle changes.

19. Close the preview and save your work.

20. Close the project.

iCONLOGiC

"Skills and Drills" Learning

Module 5: Advanced Quizzing

In This Module You Will Learn About:

And You Will Learn To:

Question Properties

In *"Articulate Storyline 3 & 360: The Essentials,"* you learned how to add a Drag and Drop Question slide to a project. During the next activity, you'll enhance a Drag and Drop Question slide by editing the question properties so that learners receive instant feedback when answering a question.

Next you'll edit the Incorrect feedback area of a question by adding an image, manipulating the feedback text, and setting branching options.

Student Activity: Modify Drag and Drop Questions

1. Open **AdvancedQuizMe** from the **Storyline3_360BeyondData** folder.

2. Open slide **3.4**.

3. Preview the slide.

4. Drag the black text boxes at the left over the clipboard images.

   Notice that as you drop the items on the clipboards, there is no indication if you've answered the question correctly or incorrectly.

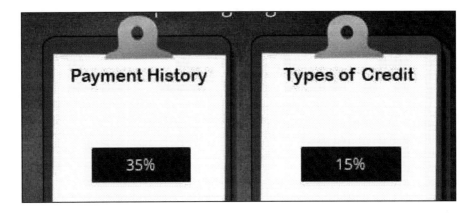

5. Click the **Submit** button and then the **Continue** button to see the feedback within the text boxes. (**Note:** You will get a Link alert because you only previewed a single slide. Click **OK** to acknowledge the alert.)

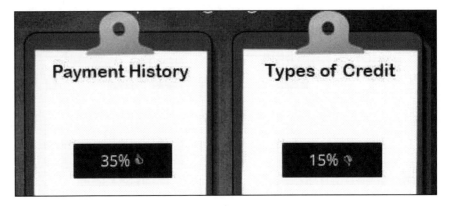

6. Close the preview.

7. Observe the current States in the project.

    ☐ on the slide, select the **35%** text box

    ☐ from the bottom of the Storyline window, click **States**

    Notice that there are three States: Normal, Drop Correct, and Drop Incorrect. Each of the text boxes on the slide has similar States. The State names are created automatically when a Drag and Drop question is inserted into a project. We edited the appearance of those States by adding a thumbs up and thumbs down symbol.

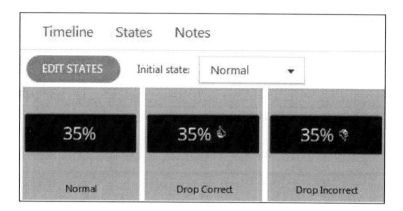

8. Set the Drag and Drop Options.

    ☐ on the **Question** panel, click **Form View**

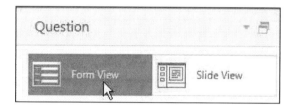

    ☐ on the **Ribbon**, notice that there is now a **Question** tab

    ☐ from the **Display** group, click **Drag & Drop Options**

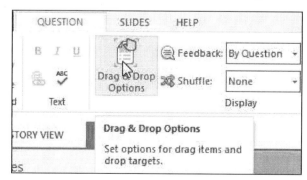

    The Drag & Drop Options dialog box opens.

❐ from the bottom of the dialog box, deselect **Delay item drop states until interaction is submitted**

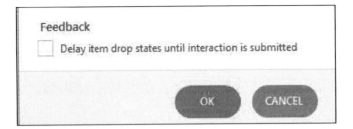

As you witnessed when you previewed the slide, when an item is dropped over a target, Storyline does not provide feedback as to whether each item has been answered correctly or incorrectly until after the learner clicks the **Submit** button. By deselecting **Delay item drop states until interaction is submitted**, the learner receives instant feedback when dragging and dropping items.

❐ click the **OK** button

9. Preview the slide.

10. Drag the black text boxes at the left over the clipboard images.

As you drop the items on the clipboard, you receive instant feedback this time.

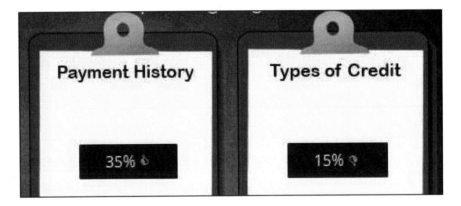

11. Close the preview.

Student Activity: Add an Image as Question Feedback

1. Ensure that the **AdvancedQuizMe** project is still open.

2. Open slide **3.3**.

3. On the **Question** panel, click **Slide View**.

4. Access the Incorrect feedback layer.

   ☐ on the **Slide Layers** panel, click **Incorrect**

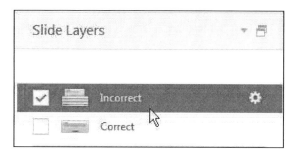

5. Insert a Picture.

   ☐ on your keyboard, press [**ctrl**] [**j**]

   The Insert Picture dialog box opens.

   ☐ from the **Storyline3_360BeyondData** folder, open the **assets** folder
   ☐ open **3.3CorrectFeedback**

   The image appears in the middle of the layer.

6. Move and resize the layer assets until the layer is similar to the image below.

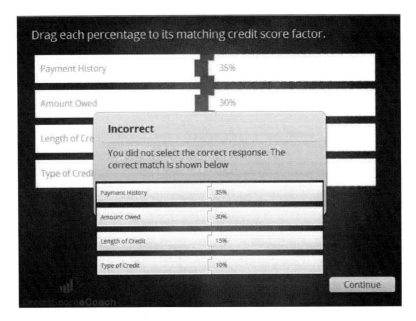

7. Preview the slide.

8. Answer the question incorrectly.

The **Incorrect** layer that you just edited should appear.

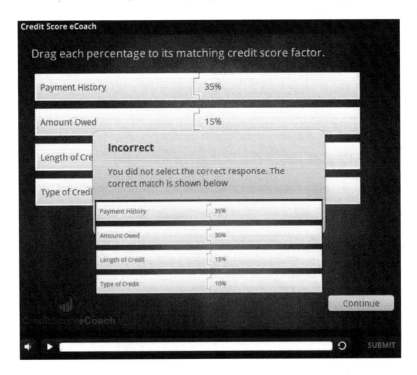

9. Close the preview.

10. Save the close the project.

Remediation

During a quiz, it's certainly possible that a learner can answer a question incorrectly. Remediation allows the learner to jump to a different part of a lesson and retrieve relevant information about the question that they answered incorrectly.

Student Activity: Set Remediation

1. Open **RemediateMe** from the **Storyline3_360BeyondData** folder.

2. Open slide **3.4**.

3. Switch to **Form View**.

4. Select a Branch for an Incorrect answer.

   ❏ from the **Set feedback and branching** area of the **Form View**, click the **More** button to the right of **Incorrect**

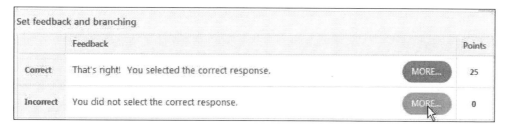

The Feedback dialog box opens.

   ❏ from the **Branch to the following** drop-down menu, choose **2.2 Factors That Affect Your Credit Score**

   ❏ click the **OK** button

Notice that there is now a Branch icon to the left of the **More** button. The Branch icon indicates that a custom Branch has been assigned.

5. Preview the entire project.

6. On the Menu, go to the **Knowledge Check** scene and select the **second** "Drag each percentage" slide.

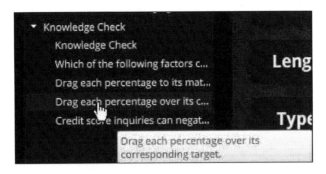

7. Answer the question incorrectly and click **Submit**.

8. Click **Continue** and, as expected, you are taken to the **Factors That Affect Your Credit Score** slide.

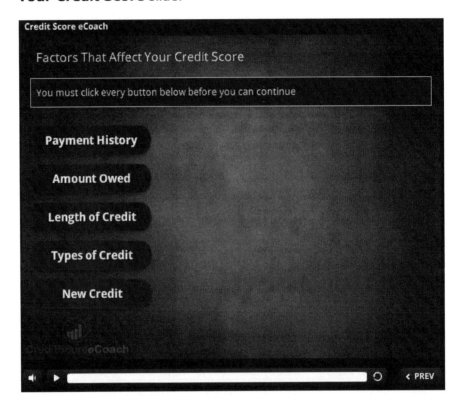

If a learner gets to this slide when working through the lesson normally, this is how the slide should look. However, if the learner gets to this slide after answering the quiz question incorrectly (as was just the case), you'd like a button to appear that allows the learner to continue with the quiz. Although this sort of behavior sounds straightforward, it requires a Variable and a few Triggers. You'll add that functionality next.

9. Close the preview.

10. Return to **Slide View** for slide **3.4**.

11. Create a Variable that allows Storyline to determine if a slide has been visited.

    ☐ on the **Triggers** panel, click **Manage project variables**

    ☐ at the bottom left of the dialog box, click **Create a new variable**

    ☐ name the **Variable questionVisited**

    ☐ change the **Type** to **True/False**

    ☐ change the **Value** to **False**

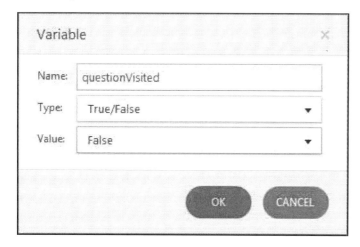

    ☐ click the **OK** button to close the **Variable** dialog box

    ☐ click the **OK** button again to close the **Variables** dialog box

12. Create a new Trigger that adjusts the questionVisited Variable, converting it from False to True.

   ☐ on the **Triggers** panel, click **Create a new trigger**

   ☐ from the **Action** drop-down menu, choose **Adjust variable**

   ☐ from the **Variable** drop-down menu, choose **questionVisited**

   ☐ from the **Operator** drop-down menu, choose **=Assignment**

   ☐ from the **Value** drop-down menu, choose **Value**

   ☐ from the next drop-down menu, choose **True**

   ☐ from the **When** drop-down menu, ensure **Timeline starts** is selected

   ☐ from the **Object** drop-down menu, ensure slide **3.4 Drag each**... is selected

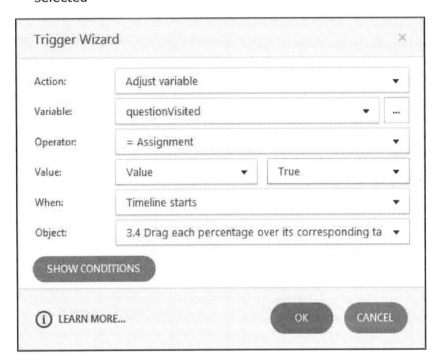

   ☐ click the **OK** button

13. Open slide **2.2**.

   Notice that there is a **Back to Quiz** button. When you select the button, you'll see that its Initial State is **Hidden**.

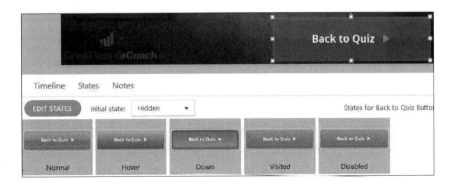

14. Add a Conditional Trigger that changes the **State** of the **Back to Quiz** button from **Hidden** to **Normal**.

    ☐ ensure that nothing on slide **2.2** is selected

    ☐ on the **Triggers** panel, click **Create a new trigger**

    ☐ from the **Action** drop-down menu, choose **Change state of**

    ☐ from the **On Object** drop-down menu, choose **Back to Quiz** button

    ☐ from the **To State** drop-down menu, choose **Normal**

    ☐ from the **When** drop-down menu, ensure **Timeline starts** is selected

Trigger Wizard		✕
Action:	Change state of	▼
On Object:	Back to Quiz Button	▼
To State:	Normal	▼
When:	Timeline starts	▼
Object:	2.2 Factors That Affect Your Credit Score	▼

SHOW CONDITIONS

ⓘ LEARN MORE...   OK   CANCEL

    ☐ click the **Show Conditions** button

    ☐ click the **Add a new condition** button (the plus sign)

    ☐ from the **If** drop-down menu, choose **questionVisited**

    ☐ from the **Operator** drop-down menu, choose **== Equal to**

    ☐ from the **Type** drop-down menu, choose **Value**

❏ from the **Value** drop-down menu, choose **True**

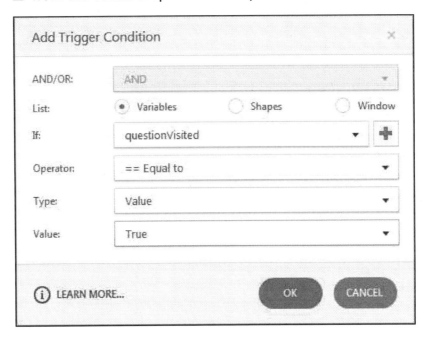

❏ click the **OK** button

❏ click the **OK** button to close the Trigger Wizard

15. Preview the entire project, enter your name when prompted, and then continue until you get to slide **2.2, Factors That Affect Your Credit Score**.

    Notice that the button does not yet appear because you have not taken the quiz.

16. On the Menu, go to the **Knowledge Check** scene and select the **second** "Drag each percentage" slide.

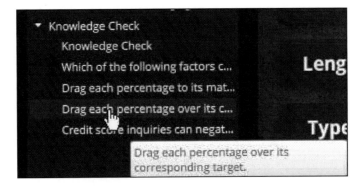

17. Answer the question incorrectly and click **Submit**.

18. Click **Continue** and you are taken back to **Factors That Affect Your Credit Score** (as expected).

    Notice that the button now appears.

19. Click the **Back to Quiz** button.

    You are taken to the next question in the quiz.

20. Close the preview.

21. Save and close the project.

Importing Question Data

To add question slides to a Storyline project, developers typically insert them via the Quizzing category on the Insert Slides dialog box. Once the questions have been added to your project, the next step is to edit the questions and answers. If you need to add a large number of question slides to a project, you will need a significant amount of time to create the quiz.

There is a better way to go, especially if the person creating the quiz does not have or use Storyline: You can import the quiz questions and answers from Excel or a text file. In the activity that follows, you'll review an Excel spreadsheet that has already been formatted with questions and answers, and then you'll import the Excel file into a Storyline project.

Student Activity: Import Questions From a File

1. Minimize Storyline and then, using **Microsoft Excel**, open **QuizData** from the **Storyline3_360BeyondData > assets** folder.

   There are two sheets in the spreadsheet: **Questions** and **Instructions**.

2. Review the Instructions.

   ❏ at the bottom of the spreadsheet, click the **Instructions** tab

   This area of the spreadsheet includes information on how to populate data on the Questions sheet prior to importing the file into Storyline.

3. Review the Questions.

   ❏ at the bottom of the spreadsheet, click the **Questions** tab

   This area of the spreadsheet is where you'll add the actual question data. During the import process, Storyline imports the data only from this sheet.

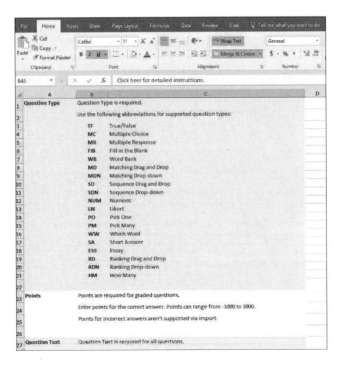

4. Close the Excel document and return to Storyline.

5. Using Storyline, open **QuizImportMe** from the **Storyline3_360BeyondData** folder.

6. Import questions from a file into a new Scene.

   ☐ on the **Slides** tab of the Ribbon, **Slide** group, click **Import** and then choose **Import Questions**

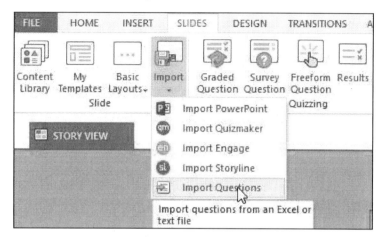

   ☐ from the **Storyline3_360BeyondData > assets** folder, open **QuizData**

   The data from the Excel file is shown in the Insert Slides dialog box. You can exclude data by deselecting the appropriate **Import** check box.

   ☐ from the **Insert into scene** drop-down menu, ensure **New scene** is selected

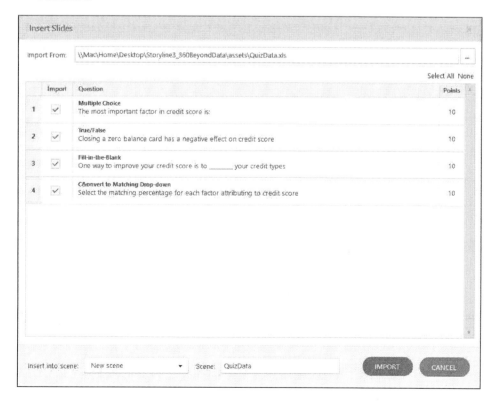

☐ click the **Import** button

A new scene named **QuizData** has been added to the project.

7. Move slides from one scene to another.

☐ select all of the slides in the **QuizData** scene

☐ drag the slides into the Knowledge Check scene (after slide 3.5)

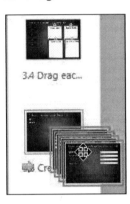

8. Delete the empty QuizData scene.

9. Save and close the project.

Random Quizzes

Creating a random quiz begins with Question Banks. By default, a Storyline project already contains a single, empty Question Bank. You can create as many banks as you need. The more Question Banks you have and the more question slides you have in each bank, the more random your quiz can be.

Student Activity: Create a Random Quiz

1. Open **QuestionBankMe** from the **Storyline3_360BeyondData** folder.

2. Edit a Question Bank.

   ❑ ensure that you are in **Story View** (no slides should be open)

   ❑ click the **Home** tab of the Ribbon

   ❑ from the **Scenes** group, click **Question Banks** and then choose **Question Bank 1**

   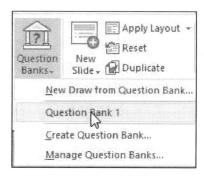

   ❑ click **import questions already in this project**

   The Import Questions dialog box opens.

   ❑ from the top of the dialog box, choose **Story** from the **Import from** drop-down menu

   ❑ from the **Import** drop-down menu, choose **Move questions into question bank**

   You could also elect to **copy the questions into the question bank**. If you go with that option, you will end up with duplicate question slides. However, that option leaves the Scene intact and allows you to re-purpose the Scene later for many different uses.

❒ from the Knowledge Check scene, select slides **13** through **16**

12	☐		**True/False** 3.5 Credit score inquiries can negatively affect your credit score.
13	✓		**Multiple Choice** 3.6 The most important factor in credit score is:
14	✓		**True/False** 3.7 Closing a zero balance card has a negative effect on credit score
15	✓		**Fill-in-the-Blank** 3.8 One way to improve your credit score is to _____ your credit types.
16	✓		**Matching Drop-down** 3.9 Select the matching percentage for each factor attributing to credit score

❒ click the **OK** button

3. Close the Question Bank.

4. Draw a question from a Question Bank randomly.

❒ while in **Story View**, select (don't open) slide **2.1** (within the Credit eCoach scene)

❒ select the **Slides** tab on the Ribbon

❒ from the **Quizzing** category, click **Question Banks** and then choose **New Draw From Question Bank**

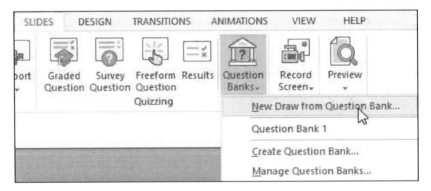

The Draw from Bank dialog box opens.

❒ ensure **Draw questions randomly** is selected

❏ from the **Include** drop-down menu, choose **2**

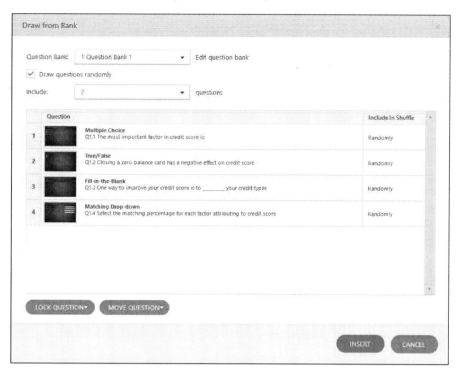

❏ click the **Insert** button

The slide group **2.2 Draw from Question Bank 1** has been added to the scene.

Random Quiz Confidence Check

1. Preview the Credit eCoach scene.

2. Click the **Next** button to see the first question. Answer the question and click the **Submit** button to see the second question.

3. Close the preview.

4. Select slide **3.5** (within the Knowledge Check scene).

5. Insert two random questions into the scene from the Question Bank.

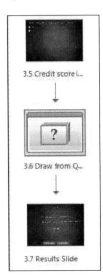

6. Save and close the project.

Quiz Result Redirection

Based on the results of a quiz, it's possible for you to send learners to different locations within your eLearning lesson. For example, when learners pass the quiz, they might end up on a congratulatory slide. However, when learners fail the quiz, they can be directed to a slide within the same scene, a slide in a different scene, a different published file, a PDF, or a website offering additional learning content.

Student Activity: Redirect a Quiz

1. Open **RedirectMe** from the **Storyline3_360BeyondData** folder.

2. Within Story View, observe **Scene 5, Quiz Results Redirects**.

   Slide **5.1** is the slide learners see when they pass the quiz. Slide **5.2** is the slide learners see when they fail the quiz.

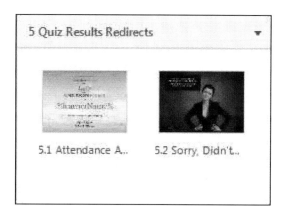

3. Open slide **3.7**.

   This is the quiz results slide. The slide has two layers: Success and Failure. You'll visit the Success slide layer and add a button that takes learners to slide 5.1. Then you'll add a button to the Failure layer that takes learners to slide 5.2.

4. Add a button (and a Trigger) to the Success layer that takes learners to slide 5.1 when they pass the quiz.

   ❏ on the **Slide Layers** panel, click the **Success** layer

   ❏ from the **Inset** tab on the Ribbon, **Interactive Objects** group, click **Button**

   ❏ choose the second button in the list

☐ draw a button on the slide similar to the image below (add the words **Get Your Certificate** as shown)

☐ create a **new Trigger**

☐ from the **Action** drop-down menu, choose **Jump to slide**

☐ from the **Slide** drop-down menu, choose **5.1 Attendance Award**

☐ from the **When** drop-down menu, ensure **User clicks** is selected

☐ from the **Object** drop-down menu, ensure **Button 1** is selected

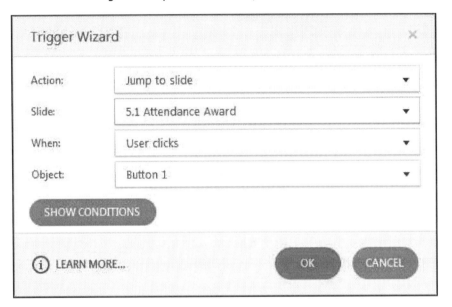

☐ click the **OK** button

Redirection Confidence Check

1. Add a button (and a Trigger) to the Failure layer that takes learners to slide 5.2 when they fail the quiz.

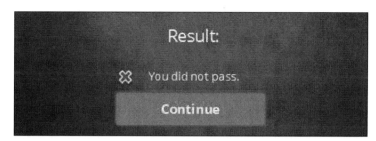

2. On the **Home** tab, click **Player** (from the **Publish** group).

3. Click **Menu** and select **Quiz Results Redirects**.

4. Click the **Trash** icon at the bottom of the dialog box. (Click the **Remove** button when prompted.)

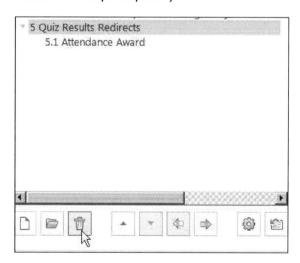

By removing the Scene from the Menu, learners won't accidentally see the redirect slides until *after* they take the quiz.

5. Preview the project and fill in your name when prompted and click the **Continue** button.

6. Go through the lesson and answer the questions as they appear. (If you pass the quiz, you should end up on slide 5.1 (with the Certificate already filled out with your name); if you fail, you should end up on slide 5.2.)

7. Close the preview and then save and close the project.

Notes

iCONLOGiC

"Skills and Drills" Learning

Module 6: Extending Storyline

In This Module You Will Learn About:

And You Will Learn To:

JavaScript

As you have seen while working through the modules in this book, you can use Triggers to perform robust interactivity and calculations. However, Triggers will take you only so far. Storyline can go beyond its built-in functionality by employing JavaScript. JavaScript is a standard scripting language used by web developers to create interactive web-based content.

Storyline allows you to execute JavaScript in your projects that perform several useful functions. For instance, you can attach a JavaScript to a button that allows learners to print a slide. You can also use a JavaScript to save project variables from a Storyline lesson into a text file. Once the data has been saved into a text file, you can import it into a database or spreadsheet.

> **Note:** According to the Articulate Storyline support documentation, JavaScript Triggers are supported in Flash and HTML5 published output. However, JavaScript isn't supported in the Articulate Mobile Player app.

Student Activity: Execute a Print JavaScript

1. Open **JavaScriptMe** from the **Storyline3_360BeyondData** folder.

2. Open slide **5.1**.

3. Execute JavaScript that allows learners to print a single slide.

   ❏ select the **Print** button on the slide

   ❏ create a new **Trigger**

   ❏ from the **Action** drop-down menu, choose **Execute JavaScript**

   ❏ from the **Script** area, click **Add/Edit JavaScript** (the three dots)

   The JavaScript dialog box opens. This is where you can type the JavaScript, paste it if you have already copied it to the clipboard, or link to it if the script is located externally. If you prefer to keep your JavaScripts external (in a separate js file), place the JavaScript file in the story_content folder of your published output. Then, add the following line of code to the story.html file before the closing </head> tag: <script LANGUAGE="JavaScript1.2">.

   ❏ type **window.print();**

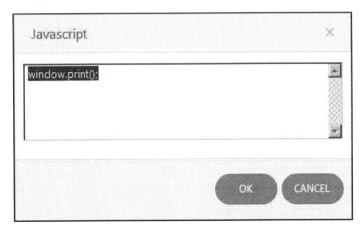

The script you just typed is about as simple as JavaScript gets. The word "window" is a browser object that calls the current browser window. The word "print" is a method that calls the browser print functionality. When you call a method you often need an array (arrays go between the open and closed parentheses). In this instance, there are no arrays needed but the parentheses are still required (even if empty).

❒ click the **OK** button twice to close both dialog boxes

4. Preview the slide.

5. Click the **Print** button.

   The JavaScript executes. However, instead of seeing the Print dialog box, you get the alert dialog box shown below. (You'd have to publish the project and work through the entire lesson to see the actual Print dialog box.)

6. Click the **OK** button to dismiss the dialog box.

7. Close the preview and then save your work.

JavaScript Confidence Check

1. Add a text box **on any slide** with the following text:

   A text Variable exists in the project named SystemDate. You are going to add a JavaScript that retrieves the current date from your computer and assigns it to this variable. You want the script to execute when the Timeline starts.

2. Minimize Storyline

3. Using Windows Explorer, open **Storyline3_360BeyondData**, **assets** and then open **systemDate.js** with Notepad.

4. Select and copy **all of the text** in the file.

5. Close the file and return to Storyline.

6. Make a new **Execute JavaScript** Trigger that uses the JavaScript you copied. (Ensure that the Trigger executes when the Timeline starts.)

```
JavaScript

var currentTime = new Date()
var month = currentTime.getMonth() + 1
var day = currentTime.getDate()
var year = currentTime.getFullYear()
var dateString=month + "/" + day + "/" + year
var player = GetPlayer();
player.SetVar("SystemDate",dateString);
```

OK   CANCEL

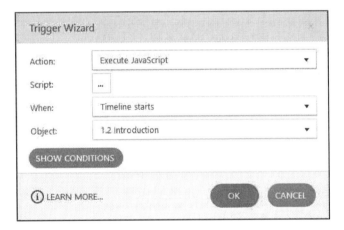

Trigger Wizard

Action:	Execute JavaScript ▼
Script:	...
When:	Timeline starts ▼
Object:	1.2 Introduction ▼

SHOW CONDITIONS

ⓘ LEARN MORE...   OK   CANCEL

7. Publish the project for the **Web**.

8. View the published project any web browser (if prompted, allow the blocked content).

The current date should appear in the upper right of your slide.

Today's Date: 5/22/2017

9. Close the browser and return to Storyline.

10. Save and close the project.

SCORM Cloud

Most eLearning content is published and then uploaded to a Learning Management System (LMS) for reporting on such things as learner access to the course, tracking, and completion. To store and track data, most LMSs use an industry standard known as SCORM. In the activities that follow, you will add a JavaScript to a lesson that will report data to and from an LMS. To test the results without having to use your own LMS, you will set up a free LMS account using SCORM Cloud. (SCORM Cloud is a cloud-based LMS that can be used for testing purposes or, if you subscribe to the service, serve as a full-featured LMS.)

Student Activity: Communicate with an LMS via a JavaScript

1. Test an existing JavaScript on an LMS.

   ☐ using any web browser, go to **http://bit.ly/2q3kwWk**

   The shortcut above will take you to an LMS on the SCORM Cloud that we have already set up for you.

   You are taken to a standard enrollment form that was automatically created by SCORM Cloud.

   ☐ type your email address into the **Email** field

   ☐ type your first and last name into the appropriate fields

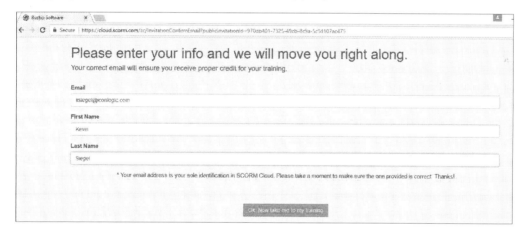

   ☐ click the **OK. Now take me to my training** button

   You will see a Popup Blocked message.

   ☐ click the **Launch Course** button

   This is a simple Storyline project that you will be working with shortly. This one already has the JavaScripts necessary to communicate with the LMS.

   ☐ click the **LMS API Full Name** button

   ☐ click the **LMS API ID** button

   ☐ click the **LMS API Split Name** button

Using JavaScript, information is retrieved from the LMS and formatted.

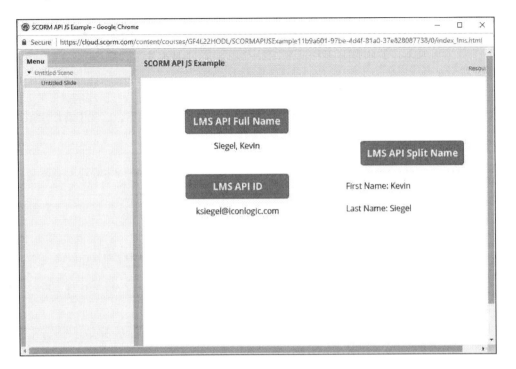

2. Close the browser and return to Storyline.

3. Open **ScormJavaScriptMe** from the **Storyline3_360BeyondData** folder.

   You are going to be executing three JavaScripts that will communicate with an LMS. Two of the scripts will retrieve enrollment information (specifically the learner's full name and email address). A third script will format the information so that it shows the learner's first and then last name (instead of last name, first name which is a SCORM standard).

4. Review existing project variables.

 ☐ on the **Triggers** panel, click **Manage project variables**

Notice that the project already contains four variables. You learned how to create and manage Variables during previous lessons in this book. This variables will referenced by the JavaScripts you are about to create.

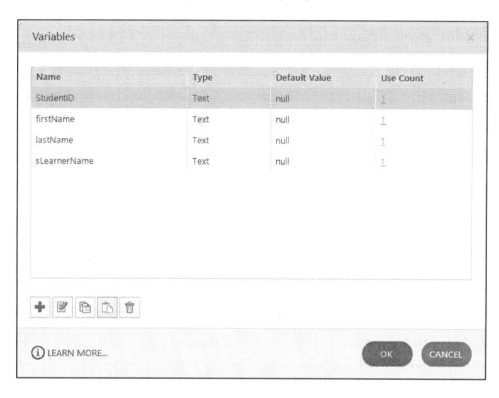

 ☐ click the **Cancel** button

5. Create a JavaScript that will retrieve the learner's full name from the LMS.

 ☐ on the slide, select the **LMS API Full Name** button
 ☐ on the **Triggers** panel, click **Add trigger**

The Trigger Wizard opens.

 ☐ from the **Action** drop-down menu, choose **Execute JavaScript**
 ☐ from the **Script** area, click the **three dots**
 ☐ in the JavaScript area, type the following:

  var player=GetPlayer();

This line makes the connection between Storyline's own JavaScript and your JavaScript.

 ☐ press [**enter**] and then type:

  player.SetVar("sLearnerName", lmsAPI.GetStudentName());

This line gets the student's name from the LMS and sets it to the Storyline variable 'sLearnerName' with the value stored within the LMS.

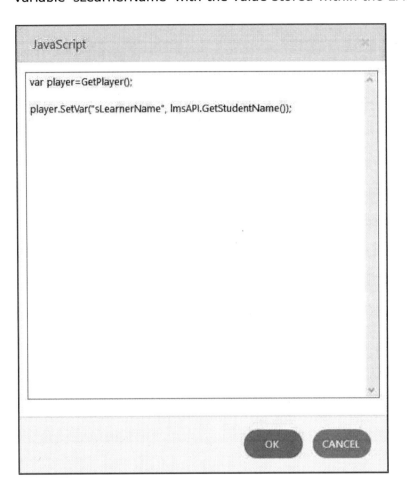

❏ click the **OK** button

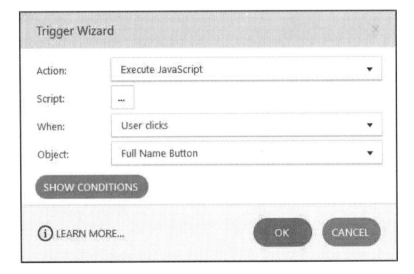

❏ click the **OK** button

6. Create a JavaScript that will retrieve the learner's ID (their email address).

   ❑ on the slide, select the **LMS API ID** button

   ❑ on the **Triggers** panel, click **Add trigger**

   The Trigger Wizard reopens.

   ❑ from the **Action** drop-down menu, choose **Execute JavaScript**

   ❑ from the **Script** area, click the **three dots**

   ❑ in the JavaScript area, type the following:

   var player=GetPlayer();

   This line makes the connection between Storyline's own JavaScript and your JavaScript.

   ❑ press [**enter**] and then type:

   player.SetVar("StudentID", lmsAPI.GetStudentID());

   This line gets the student's ID from the LMS and sets it to the Storyline variable 'StudentID' with the value stored within the LMS.

❑ click the **OK** button

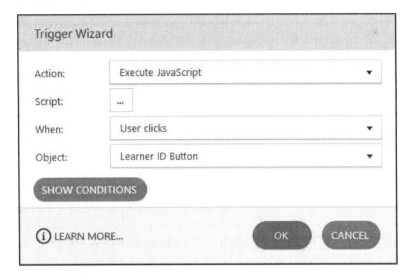

❑ click the **OK** button

7. Create a third JavaScript that will format the name as first and then last.

❑ on the slide, select the **LMS API Split Name** button

❑ on the **Triggers** panel, click **Add trigger**

The Trigger Wizard reopens.

❑ from the **Action** drop-down menu, choose **Execute JavaScript**

❑ from the **Script** area, click the **three dots**

❑ in the JavaScript area, type the following:

```
var player = GetPlayer();
var myName = lmsAPI.GetStudentName();
var array = myName.split(',');
var firstName = array[1];
var lastName = array[0];
if( firstName.charAt( 0 ) === ' ' )
      firstName = firstName.slice( 1 );
player.SetVar("firstName", firstName);
player.SetVar("lastName", lastName);
```

The first line (**var player**) makes the connection between Storyline's own JavaScript and your JavaScript.

The next line (**var myName**) creates a new variable in the JavaScript named **myName** and assigns to it the full name value from the LMS.

The next line (**var array**) creates an array that splits the name into two values at the comma.

The **var firstName** line takes the second value from the array and stores it in the Storyline **firstName** variable.

The **var lastName** line takes the first value from the array and stores it in the Storyline **lastName** variable.

The **if(firstName.charAt(0) === ' ')** line removes the space if it appears after the comma.

The last two lines assign the first and last names from the JavaScript to the Storyline variables.

```
JavaScript                                                    ✕

var player = GetPlayer();

var myName  = lmsAPI.GetStudentName();

var array  = myName.split(',');

var firstName = array[1];

var lastName = array[0];

if( firstName.charAt( 0 ) === ' ' )
    firstName = firstName.slice( 1 );

player.SetVar("firstName", firstName);

player.SetVar("lastName", lastName);



                                         OK        CANCEL
```

❏ click the **OK** button

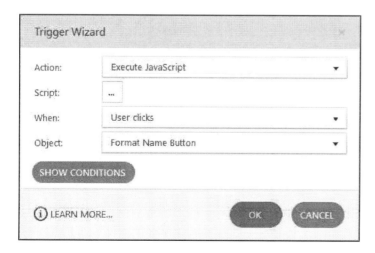

```
Trigger Wizard                                                ✕

Action:      Execute JavaScript                          ▼

Script:      ...

When:        User clicks                                 ▼

Object:      Format Name Button                          ▼

   SHOW CONDITIONS

ⓘ LEARN MORE...                          OK        CANCEL
```

❏ click the **OK** button

8. Save your work.

Note: You already tested the finished JavaScript in our existing SCORM Cloud account. However, if you want to test this on your own, you will first need to create a free SCORM Cloud account (**https://scorm.com/scorm-solved/scorm-cloud-features**) or work with your existing LMS. You would then publish the project as a SCORM package and upload it into your LMS.

iCONLOGiC

"Skills and Drills" Learning

Module 7: Accessibility and Reporting

In This Module You Will Learn About:

And You Will Learn To:

Accessibility

You can use Storyline to create eLearning lessons that are accessible to users who have visual, hearing, mobility, or other types of disabilities. If you publish Flash content (SWF), the content can be made compliant. However, HTML5 and Articulate Mobile Player output isn't currently compliant.

The World Wide Web Consortium (W3C) publishes the Web Content Accessibility Guidelines, a document that specifies what developers should do to their content to make it accessible. Today, many countries, including the United States, Australia, Canada, Japan, and countries in Europe, have adopted accessibility standards based on those developed by the W3C.

In the United States, the law that governs accessibility is commonly known as Section 508. Part of the Rehabilitation Act of 1973, Section 508 requires that federal agencies and federally funded organizations, such as colleges and universities, develop or use information technology that is accessible to people with disabilities.

Generally speaking, eLearning is considered accessible if it can be used by a learner who does not have to rely on a single sense or ability. Learners should be able to move through lessons using only a keyboard or a mouse. In addition, the lessons should include visual and auditory elements to support both hearing and visually impaired learners.

Your published Storyline lessons can be read by a screen reader. Screen readers are programs that use auditory feedback to read screen information to a learner. In addition, the screen reader acts as a mouse pointer, providing navigation via keyboard commands.

The most widely used screen readers are separate commercial products: JAWS from Freedom Scientific, Window-Eyes from GW Micro, Dolphin Supernova by Dolphin, System Access from Serotek, and ZoomText Magnifier/Reader from AiSquared are prominent examples in the English-speaking market. The open source screen reader NVDA is gaining popularity.

The following Storyline elements can be made accessible:

- ☐ Images

- ☐ Slide text

- ☐ Slide names

- ☐ Buttons

- ☐ Playback controls (The function of each button is read by screen readers.)

- ☐ Slide transcripts using the Notes tab

- ☐ Question slides (Some Question slides are not considered accessible. Multiple choice and true/false are the easiest for a visually impaired learner to navigate.)

- ☐ Voiceover audio via closed captions

You can learn more about Section 508 by visiting www.section508.gov. And you can learn more about Storyline and Accessibility by visiting the Articulate website articulate.com/support/article/Articulate-Storyline-and-Section-508-Accessibility.

Student Activity: Make an Image Accessible

1. Open **AccessibilityMe** from the **Storyline3_360BeyondData** folder.

2. Open slide **1.2**.

3. Make a picture accessible.

   ❑ on the **Timeline**, select **Picture3**

   ❑ on the far right of the Ribbon's **Format** tab, click the **Size** drop-down menu

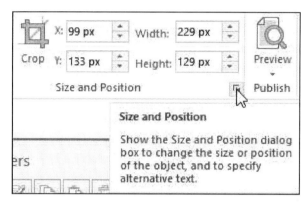

The Size and Position dialog box open.

   ❑ from the left of the dialog box, select **Accessibility**

   ❑ in the Alternate text field, type **Woman holding a tablet with credit score information.**

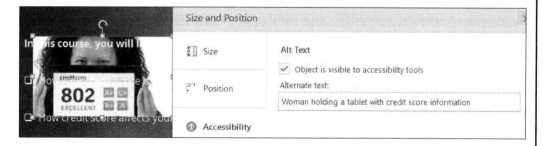

When an assistive device comes across an object with Alternative Text, the assistive device reads the text aloud for the learner. To hear the Alternative Text, the learners have to first enable the accessibility features of their computer or device.

   ❑ click the **Close** button

Note: The slide also contains text boxes and a text button. The text you see is automatically read aloud by assistive devices.

Image Accessibility Confidence Check

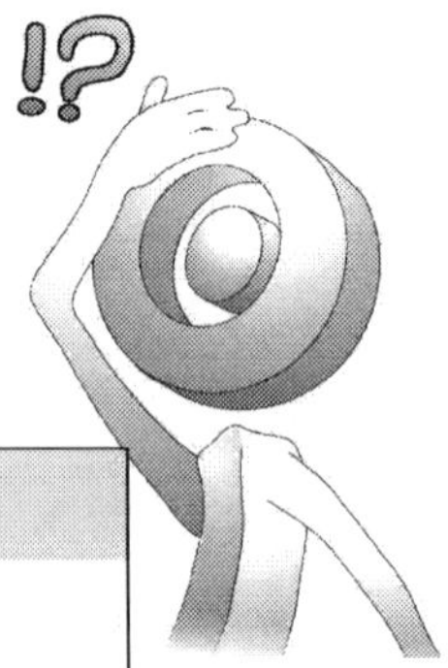

1. Still working on slide **1.2** of the **AccessibilityMe** project, add the following Alternate text to the remaining three images.

   Picture4: Calculator with a financial statement

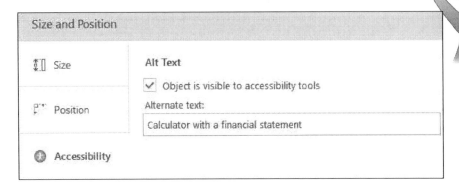

   Picture5: House on top of a mountain of cash

   Picture6: Various credit and debit cards

2. Open slide **1.1**.

3. On the Timeline, select **Video1**.

4. Add the following Alternate text: **Woman walks across the screen, faces you, and welcomes you to the lesson.**

5. Save your work.

Student Activity: Control Accessibility Visibility

1. Ensure that **AccessibilityMe** it still open.

2. Open slide **2.4**.

3. Make an object invisible to accessibility tools.

   ☐ on the **Timeline**, select **Group 1**

   ☐ on far right of the **Format** tab, click the **Size** drop-down menu

   ☐ from the left of the dialog box, select **Accessibility**

   ☐ at the top of the dialog box, deselect **Object is visible to Accessibility tools**

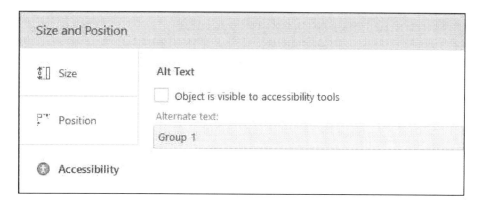

With the Object is visible to Accessibility tools option deselected, the selected group (which isn't important enough to have the accessibility device read to the learner), is ignored by the reader.

   ☐ click the **Close** button

Tab Order

Learners can select screen objects on a slide by either clicking the mouse or using the [**tab**] key on the keyboard. By default, the Tab Order is determined by the order by which you added objects to the slide. The first object added is the first object in the Tab Order. You can easily edit a slide's Tab Order prior to publishing your project.

Student Activity: Edit the Tab Order

1. Ensure that **AccessibilityMe** it still open.

2. Open slide **2.3**.

3. Preview the slide.

   Press the [**tab**] on your keyboard and notice that the **Length of Credit** button is the first thing that gets selected. You are going to edit the Tab Order and ensure that the **Length of Credit** button gets selected much later.

4. Close the preview.

5. Create a custom tab order.

6. Reset the Tab Order.

   ❏ ensure that nothing on the slide is selected

   ❏ on the **Home** tab of the Ribbon, **Slide** group, click **Tab Order**

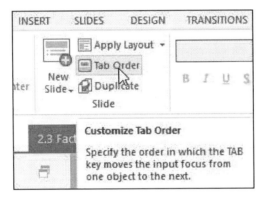

The Tab Order dialog box opens.

   ❏ if necessary, select **Create custom tab order**

   ❏ from the **Shape** column, select the **first item**

❏ on the bottom right of the dialog box, click **Move the selected shape down in the tab order** several times to move the item to **bottom of the list**

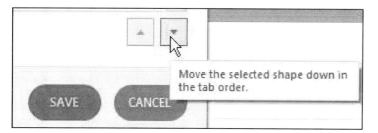

❏ click the **Save** button

7. Preview the slide.

Press the [**tab**] on your keyboard and notice that the Length of Credit button is no longer the first thing that gets selected.

8. Reset the Tab Order.

❏ ensure that nothing on the slide is selected

❏ on the **Home** tab of the Ribbon, **Slide** group, click **Tab Order**

The Tab Order dialog box reopens.

❏ from the bottom of the dialog box, click **Reset Order**

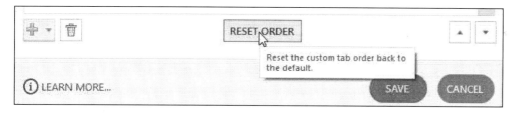

❏ click the **Save** button

9. Preview the slide.

Press [**tab**] on your keyboard and notice that this time objects on the slide are selected from top to bottom (which makes sense from a usability standpoint).

10. Close the preview.

Keys

By default, the [enter] triggers interactive areas of a Storyline project. However, if you want to change the keyboard shortcut, it's good to know that you can easily assign any keyboard you like to interactive objects.

Although you can use just about any keyboard shortcut or combination of keys as your shortcut keys, you should carefully test those shortcuts in several web browsers. Some keyboard shortcuts are reserved by the browser. The keys might work as expected when you preview the lesson from within Storyline. However, when you preview the lesson in a browser, the keys might be intercepted by the web browser and not work as expected. (For instance, the [F1] key historically displays the Help window, so you should avoid it in Storyline.)

Student Activity: Add a Keyboard Shortcut to a Button

1. Ensure that **AccessibilityMe** it still open.

2. Open slide **2.5**.

3. Assign a keyboard shortcut to activate an interactive object.

   ❐ on the **Timeline**, select **Rectangle 1** (this is a transparent rectangle that is linked to slide 4.1)

   ❐ create a new Trigger

   ❐ from the **Action** drop-down menu, choose **Lightbox slide**

   ❐ from the **Slide** drop-down menu, choose **4.1 Credit Score Calculator**

   ❐ from the **When** drop-down menu, choose **User presses a key**

   ❐ in the **Key** field, type **R**

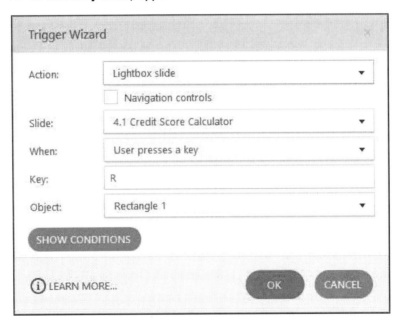

   ❐ click the **OK** button

4. Preview the project.

5. From the **Menu** at the left, click **Credit Score Resources**.

6. On your keyboard, press the [**tab**] until the rectangle in the middle of the slide is selected.

7. On your keyboard, press **r** to display the content from slide 4.1.

8. Close the preview.

Closed Captioning

Closed captioning allows you to display a slide's voiceover audio as text that is synchronized with the voiceover audio. Closed Captions, which are an expected component of an accessible eLearning lesson, are easy to include in your project. All that you need to do is select an audio file on the Timeline and import either an SRT (a file containing text and timing information), VTT, SBV, or SUB file. You can learn more about each of these file formats and how to create them with a simple Web search. For instance, a free SRT file can easily be created from a YouTube video. You can learn more about the SRT format and how to utilize YouTube via https:// community.articulate.com/series/74/articles/articulate-storyline-360-user-guide-how-to-add-closed-captions). We know, that's a long link. We've shortened it here for your convenience: http://bit.ly/2rQbuJr.

To proceed with Captioning, you will need an audio file and a text file such as an SRT. Given that you probably don't have either, we've saved you the trouble by including an SRT file in the **Storyline3_360BeyondData** folder (**captions.srt**) that matches an audio file that we've also provided. After importing the SRT file (it's just a few clicks), you'll learn how to format the resulting Closed Captions.

Student Activity: Add Captions

1. Open **CloseCaptionMe** from the **Storyline3_360BeyondData** folder.

2. Open slide **1.1**.

3. Import an SRT file onto an audio object.vt

   ☐ on the **Timeline**, select **Audio 1**

   ☐ on the **Options** tab of the **Ribbon**, **Closed Captions** area, click **Import**

replace shot p162A

   ☐ from **Storyline3_360BeyondData folder > assets > audio**, open **captions.srt**

And that's it. Closed captions from the SRT file have been added and synchronized with the audio on slide 1.

4. Preview the slide and notice that a Closed Captions control has been automatically added to the Player. (You can disable the Closed Captions control via the **Player Properties > Controls** area shown in the second image below.)

5. Click the **Closed Captions control** and you'll see the captions.

6. Close the Preview.

7. Change the font used in the Closed Captions.

   ❏ on the **Ribbon**, click **Player Properties**

   ❏ click **Colors & Effects**

   ❏ from the **Captions font** drop-down menu, choose any font you like

   ❏ click the **OK** button

8. Preview the slide and click the Closed Captions control to see the new font in the captions.

9. Close the Preview.

   By default, the closed captions were not displayed when you previewed. In the next activity, you will learn how to change the default so that the captions display automatically.

Student Activity: Show the Closed Captions By Default

1. Ensure that the **CloseCaptionMe** project is still open.

2. Open slide **1.1**.

3. Modify a variable so that the closed captions display automatically.

   ☐ on the **Triggers** panel, click **Manage project variables**

   The first variable in the list is called **Player.DisplayCaptions**. This variable was automatically created the instant you imported the SRT file earlier. By default, it is set to hide the captions when the lesson is opened by the learner.

   ☐ in the Default Value column, click the word **False** and choose **True** from the drop-down menu

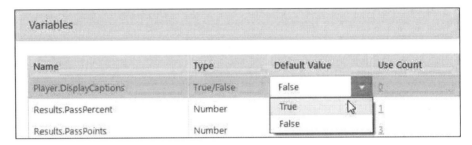

   ☐ click the **OK** button

4. Preview the slide notice that the captions appear automatically.

5. Close the Preview.

6. Save and close the project.

Reporting

Later in this module you will publish a project and then upload it into an LMS (using an LMS called Articulate Online). Prior to working with a typical LMS, you have to set up some reporting options and specify the Sharable Content Object Reference Model (SCORM) version standard, Aviation Industry Computer-Based Training Committee (AICC), Sharable Content Object (SCO), and the Manifest File. However, Articulate Online is simple and takes many of the Storyline settings into account automatically.

Sharable Content Object Reference Model

Developed by public- and private-sector organizations, SCORM is a series of eLearning standards that specifies ways to catalog, launch, and track course objects. Courses and management systems that follow the SCORM specifications allow for sharing of courses among federal agencies, colleges, and universities. Although SCORM is not the only eLearning standard (AICC is another), SCORM is one of the most common. There are two primary versions of SCORM—version 1.2, released in 1999, and version 2004.

During the remaining activities in this module, you will prepare and then publish a project to a SCORM-compliant LMS.

Aviation Industry Computer-Based Training Committee

AICC is an international association that develops guidelines for the aviation industry in the development, delivery, and evaluation of training technologies. When you publish your Captivate projects, you can specify SCORM or AICC compliance, but not both. Not sure which one to pick? Talk to your LMS provider for information on which one to use. When in doubt, consider that AICC is older and more established than SCORM, but SCORM is the standard most often used today.

Tin Can API

Today's learners are consuming eLearning content using a vast array of devices (PCs, Macs, and mobile devices such as the iPad). And learners are working outside of traditional LMSs. In spite of these challenges, educators still need to capture reliable data about the learner experience.

The problem with data collection is that you need an expensive LMS to store the data. And your learners need live access to the LMS so that they can send the data. As mentioned above, the most widely used LMS standard for capturing data is SCORM. SCORM allows educators to track things such as learner completion of a course, pass/fail rates, and the amount of time a learner takes to complete a lesson or course. But what if a trainer needs to get scores from learners who are collaborating with other students using social media? What if the learners don't have access to the Internet?

The new Tin Can API allows training professionals to gather detailed data about the learner experience as the learner moves through an eLearning course (either online or offline). According to the Tin Can API website, "The Tin Can API (sometimes known as the **Experience API**) captures data in a consistent format about a person or group's activities from many technologies. Very different systems are able to securely communicate by capturing and sharing this stream of activities using Tin Can's simple vocabulary."

If the Tin Can API is supported by your LMS, you'll be happy to learn that it's also fully supported in Storyline.

Sharable Content Object

SCOs are standardized, reusable learning objects. An LMS can launch and communicate with SCOs and can interpret instructions that tell the LMS which SCO to show a user and when to show it. Why should you know what an SCO is? Actually, your Storyline projects are SCOs once you enable reporting. Next, you will publish the project into a Content Package so that it can be uploaded into an LMS.

Student Activity: Upload a Project to an LMS

1. Open **LMSme** from the **Storyline3_360BeyondData** folder.

2. Create an Articulate Online account.

   ❏ choose **File > Publish**

   ❏ select **Articulate Online**

   ❏ if you don't already have an Articulate Online account, from the bottom of the dialog box, click **Start your FREE Articulate Online trial now**

The Articulate download page opens.

   ❏ click the **Try Free** button

   ❏ follow the onscreen instructions to set up your trial account for **Articulate Online**

Pay particular attention to the Account URL. You will need that URL in Storyline soon.

   ❏ return to Storyline and the **LMSme** project

3. Publish content to Articulate Online.

☐ in the **Account URL** field, enter the URL you used when activating the Articulate Online account

☐ type your email address and password into the appropriate fields

☐ click the **Publish** button

The Publish Successful dialog box opens.

☐ click the **Manage Content** button

The Articulate Online page opens with your lesson included on the **Content** tab. Using Articulate Online, you can add users, generate reports, etc. The basic expected LMS functionality is available. You can continue to upload and test your Storyline projects here for 30 days. At that point, your account becomes inactive unless you subscribe to the pay service.

☐ on the **Content** tab, click **Credit Score eCoach**

❏ click the **Launch Content** button

The lesson you created and published opens within the LMS. Congratulations, you are a published eLearning author... and you have completed this book!

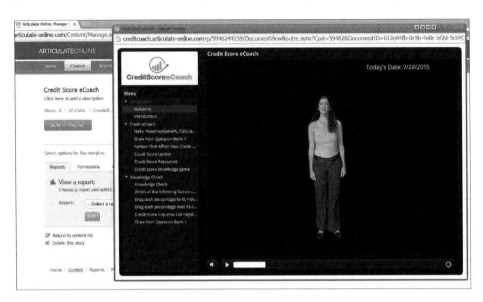

We hope you have enjoyed using this book to learn advanced features within Storyline. For more information about Storyline, visit the E-Learning Heroes website (community.articulate.com). You will find hundreds of articles, forums, downloads, and more... all free. And visit the IconLogic website (www.iconlogic.com) to subscribe to our free "skills & drills" newsletter and attend our live, interactive training classes.

Index

Made in the USA
Middletown, DE
23 April 2018